LEADERSHIP LESSONS FROM A VACUUM CLEANER !! ?? !!

LEADERSHIP LESSONS FROM A VACUUM CLEANER !! ?? !!

BY

STEPHANIE OLEXA, PhD, MBA

Leadership Lessons From A Vacuum Cleaner !! ?? !!

ISBN: 978-1-300-29416-0 (sc)

Table of Contents

Acknowledgements

This book is dedicated to the managers and leaders in business, who are actively pursuing personal excellence in their lives as well as in their careers in order to be the best they can be. This book would not have been possible without the mindful and continuous support of my husband, Seth Weber, who encouraged me through the transitions in my life and my sister, Georgine Olexa, who epitomizes intelligence and trustworthiness. I am blessed to have both of them in my life.

I am grateful to my editors, G. Patrick Gallagher and Walter L. Kleine, for their thoughtful and comprehensive reviews of my manuscript.

I would like to thank the iRobot Corporation for their support and for allowing me to use the name and image of their Roomba® robotic vacuum cleaner as the theme for this book.

If you have suggestions or questions about this book or other books in the series, contact me at www.leadtothefuture.com. I hope to hear from you.

Preface

Through my long career as a scientist, teacher, entrepreneur and now, leadership coach, I read hundreds, if not thousands of books on leadership and self-development. What I found was that I enjoyed the ones that used facts and figures to prove their points. I remembered the ones with stories that emphasized the intended message. But I used the ones that had a central theme with a way of communicating the message to others in a simple, yet visual way. I stumbled across the theme of the Roomba® vacuum cleaner while coaching two clients. With their encouragement I started writing the book and found that it gave me a simple way of tying together and communicating some of the most important life and leadership lessons that I have learned. I hope this makes you smile and think. I hope this opens new doors for you. I hope you learn to Roomba®!

Introduction

In 2008, a friend introduced me to his Roomba® robotic vacuum cleaner, made by iRobot. He swore by the product. Not only did it clean his condo effortlessly, but his pet parrot had fallen in love with it. The company was founded in 1990 by roboticists Colin Angle, Helen Greiner, and Rodney Brooks from Massachusetts Institute of Technology. They launched the robotic home vacuum cleaner in 2002, so I wasn't exactly on the cutting edge of technology, but I was intrigued. At the time, I was running a business that I had founded, doing executive and leadership coaching and trying to keep a semblance of order in our home. My mantra to my employees and coaching clients was always, "What would the lazy person do?" Not that I was encouraging slothfulness, but a lazy person would do things right the first time (too lazy to do it over again), delegate appropriately (too lazy to do it all himself/herself), streamline processes (why waste energy or time?) and work effectively on a team (share the work). The Roomba® appeared to be the perfect companion for "a lazy person."

Since Roomba® joined our family, it has worked tirelessly to keep the fur from my three cats contained and to minimize the sneezing from my allergy-prone husband. It attacks my problems (dirt, dust, and fur balls the size of tumbleweeds) with energy and determination. It solves problems! Just as Roomba® knows how to remove dirt and dust from a room, it also can teach us about removing problems and issues in our business and personal lives. But, I'm also amazed at how much it knows about success in business and in life.

Several months ago, I was coaching a client who is a high-ranking executive in a very stressful position. She also happens to be blind. As is my standard practice, I opened the coaching session with the question, "What is most important to discuss today?"

She said that she was frustrated because she was with several colleagues and had walked into a wall...literally. Although she wasn't hurt, she was embarrassed and feared that her colleagues would think that she was not competent. For a blind individual, it's not unusual to walk into immobile objects, so we discussed the difference between physical competence and intellectual competence. Finally I said to her, "You need to learn to Roomba®."

There was a long silence. Then she reminded me that blind people don't learn to dance.

"ROOMBA, NOT RUMBA!" I described my robotic vacuum cleaner and told her about how it sped across the family room, hit the wall, turned forty five degrees and sped off again. Just because it hit the wall didn't mean it was incompetent. Hitting the wall didn't slow it down. It was resilient!

A few weeks later, I was having lunch with an entrepreneur who was describing the many false starts, restarts, and reinventions that he went through to make his venture successful. Flexible, changing direction and determined to be successful, just like Roomba®.

So what other lessons can we learn? Read on.

Chapter 1

Start from where you are

I can put Roomba anywhere, in my family room, living room, guest bedroom, or kitchen. When I press the clean button, it spins in gradually increasing circles to assess the new situation. Then it takes off. It has been programmed by the geniuses at iRobot to be completely confident in a new situation, with extremely high self-esteem. But it also takes the time to assess what skills and resources it needs and can access in this new situation. It balances self-esteem with self-assessment in order to start from where it is.

So, where should you start? Start from where *you* are! To start where you are, first you need to figure out where you *really* are. That means understanding the *inside* (who you are, who you are not) and the *outside* (what resources you have or can have access to, what resources you do not have access to, and what resources you need), all in a positive but very realistic way. By balancing your self-assessment with your self-esteem, you will be in a great place to start.

Balancing self-assessment and self-esteem

In the Merriam Webster Dictionary there are 261 words that start with "self," from the ones with negative connotations, selfish, self-centered, self-absorbed, to the ones we strive for, selfless, self-assured and self-confident. It can be very confusing. If you say that you feel good about yourself, do you have self-pride (negative connotation) or self-approval (positive connotation)? If you are never satisfied with your accomplishments, are you self-critical (negative connotation) or self-motivating (positive connotation)?

In the same way, self-esteem has been shadowed with both positive and negative connotations. For today, let's focus on self-esteem with the following definition.

Self-esteem is the unconscious set of beliefs, formed over our lives, which reflect our perceptions of our abilities, our lovability and our ability to control events in our lives. It reflects our sense of belonging, feelings of competence, and our personal power to control our lives. Self-esteem is always based on the necessary and critical quality of accurate self-assessment. Self-assessment is acknowledging your strengths and weaknesses without bias, and acknowledging how the world actually sees you.

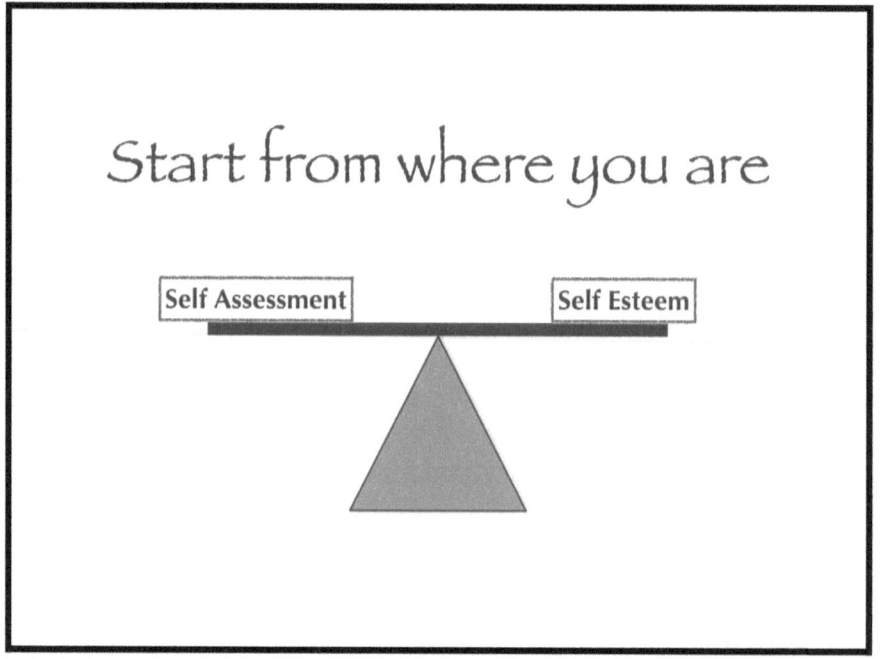

In 2009, I attended Georgetown University's certificate program on Leadership Coaching. My goal was to evolve from a business owner to a leadership and executive coach, and I thought that this intense and professional program was the way to go. I was not disappointed. Because of the excellent instructors and thoughtful colleagues in the course, I not only learned about coaching, but about myself. In preparation for the first class, we were told to bring a bound notebook or journal to use to capture our thoughts and learning through the course. So, on the first day of class I sat attentively with my black marble, $1.06 notebook. The first thing we were asked to do was to write in big letters on the first page, "I AM A GREAT COACH." And, on the second page we were instructed to write, "IN THE DOMAIN OF COACHING I AM A BEGINNER." I didn't get it. True, I was a beginner. No way was I a great coach. But I learned about positive affirmations, seeing yourself in your best moments, garnering all of your resources, and projecting yourself into the best that you can be. And, I learned about true, complete, and accurate acknowledgement of who and what I am now. In those two statements I balanced my self-esteem and self-assessment in the domain of coaching. It was a great place to start.

Alongside the definition of self-esteem in the dictionary, we can all imagine that there are pictures of the CEOs of the world's most powerful companies. CEOs rose to their positions of extreme power because they are intelligent, savvy, dedicated, and resourceful. However, the success rate and longevity of CEOs in their jobs in the past decade has declined dramatically. According to Ray Williams in his article, *Why do CEOs fail, and what can we do about it?* (Williams, 2010), global Chief Executives now have a job tenure of 7.6 years, down from 9.5 years in 1995. Further, two out of five new CEOs fail in their first eighteen months on the job. So, why do so many leading CEOs fail? Why the dramatic stories of CEO removal in the *Wall Street Journal*? Why this crisis in leadership? Williams proposes that the failures have nothing to do with competence, knowledge, or experience. He suggests that a major reason is that these leaders have a gap between how they see themselves and how others see them. The gap prevents them from being open to change, makes them resistant to opinions of others, and causes them to ignore feedback. This gap is hubris, a gap between their self-esteem and honest self-assessment.

Individuals with high self-esteem consistently rate themselves as being smarter, better looking, more accomplished, and more well-liked than their colleagues. In many cases, they are flattering themselves, and on objective assessments it's just not true. High, but undeserved, self-esteem, also known as narcissism, has become extremely prevalent in the United States today. In the book *The Narcissism Epidemic*, Twenge and Campbell (Twenge &

Campbell, 2009) describe narcissism in society as resting on a four-legged stool, each leg representing one causative element. The four legs are:

- ✓ Developmental – including permissive parenting and self-esteem focused education.
- ✓ Media culture of the shallow celebrity.
- ✓ Internet encouragement of individuals to present an inflated and self-focused view of themselves to the world and encouraging them to spend many hours a day contemplating their images.
- ✓ Easy access to credit and financial support to make narcissistic dreams into reality.

This upswing in narcissistic behavior in society today is causing a lack of leadership, particularly in the development of the next generation of leaders.

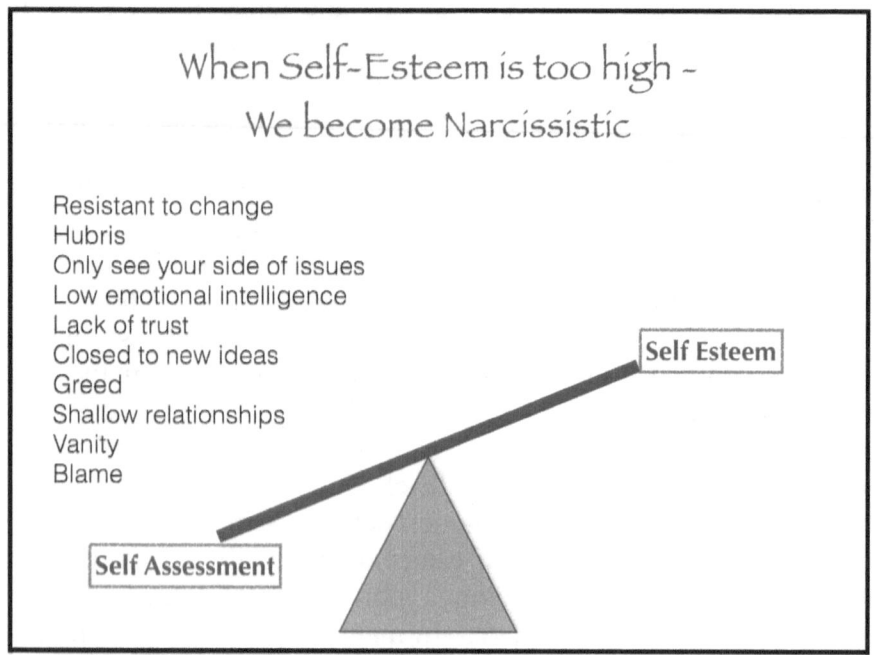

When Self-Esteem is too high –
We become Narcissistic

Resistant to change
Hubris
Only see your side of issues
Low emotional intelligence
Lack of trust
Closed to new ideas
Greed
Shallow relationships
Vanity
Blame

Self Esteem

Self Assessment

Of course, if self-esteem is low and self-assessment is high, the individual can become so self-critical that they lose confidence and also become an ineffective leader.

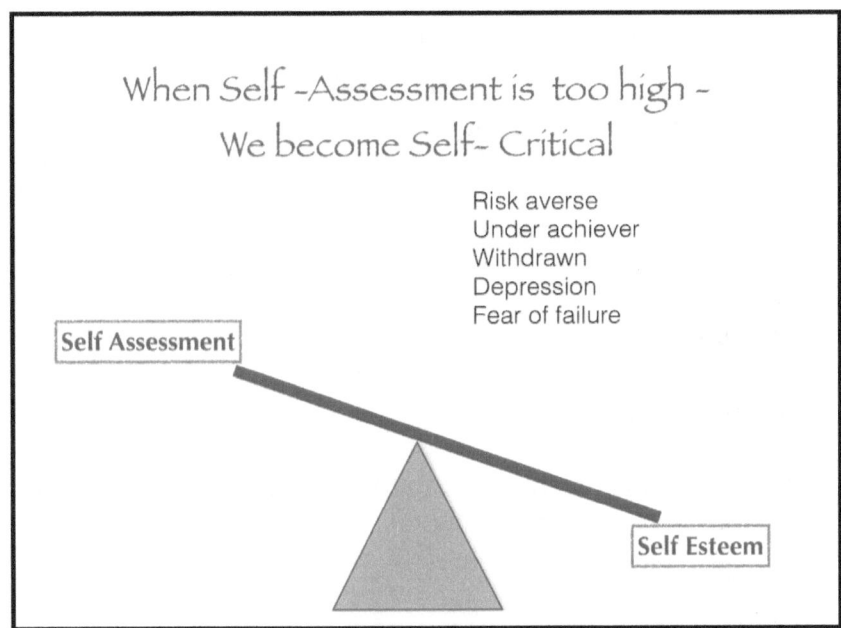

The goal is to have your self-esteem and self-assessment in balance!

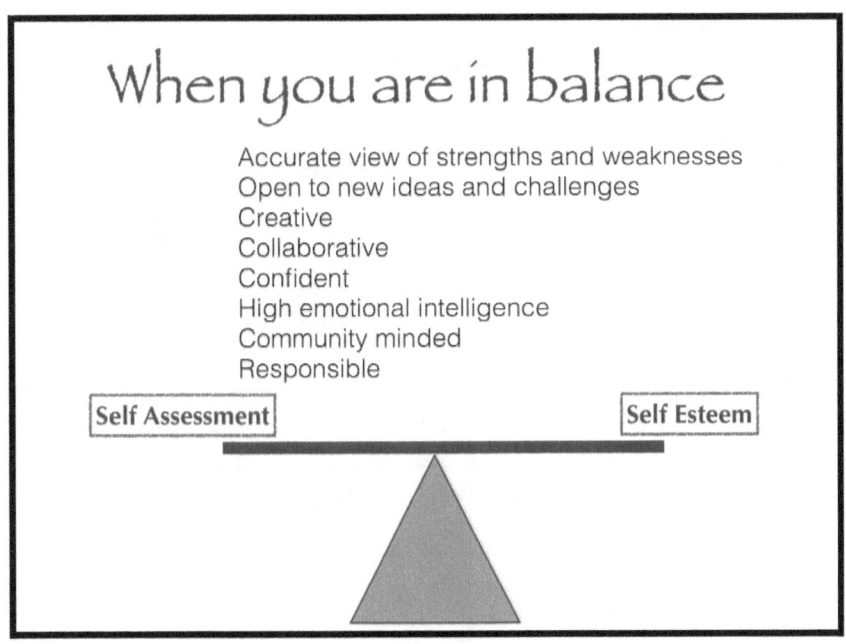

Discovering who you are and who you are not

Self-discovery is the active journey to find out who you are and who you are not. In his book, *I Am*, Howard Falco (Falco, 2010) guides the reader along the path of finding out who he or she really is, by addressing the following questions:

- ✓ What am I?
- ✓ How am I?
- ✓ Why am I?
- ✓ Who can I be?

He recommends that we follow a journey of consciously creating our lives with the following steps:

1. Ask tough questions about yourself to address the deep, and sometimes not so nice, parts of yourself to get a clear picture of where you are and what you want to be. Understand your DESIRE.
2. Accept the truth of the answers, even if it is not easy. Exert your WILL.
3. Choose who you are. Recognize that you have POWER over who you are now and who you will become.
4. Act on this belief in yourself. Have FAITH in yourself.
5. Experience the perfection of the results. LOVE yourself, ACCEPT yourself, be your own best friend, be COMPASSIONATE to yourself.

In many cases, when we ask these tough questions about ourselves, we don't want to accept the reality of the answers and it puts a hold on the process of creating who we are. We deny the answer, delude ourselves, express contempt, or judge others.

Finding Balance

To have a proper balance between self-assessment and self-esteem, you need to honestly assess your strengths and weaknesses, and then accept them with compassion.

1. Accurately identify your weaknesses.
    a. Describe your weaknesses, using neutral language, not judgmental. What objective evidence do you have that this really is a weakness? What proof do you have? Was it a one-time event or a patterned weakness?
    b. Don't exaggerate or embellish your weaknesses.
    c. Use language that is specific and not global. Remove all words such as "always" or "never."
    d. Identify when and how you have overcome these weaknesses in the past, or have a compensating strength.
    e. Identify ways that you can overcome these weaknesses in the future.
2. Accurately identify your strengths.
    a. Describe your strengths using neutral language, but do not be shy about saying good things about yourself. What objective evidence do you have that this really is a strength? What proof do you have? Was this a one-time event or a pattern of strength?
    b. Review your past successes and achievements for patterns.
    c. Describe skills you have mastered.
    d. Identify ways that you have used your strengths to achieve your goals.
    e. Identify strengths that you can enhance or build upon.
3. Accept your strengths and weaknesses with compassion.
    a. Accept all your qualities, both positive and negative.
    b. Forgive yourself for past mistakes, and don't exaggerate them into major flaws.

    c. Accept that in the past you made the best decisions that you could at the time based on the information you had. You may not make the same decision now with new information, but that does not change the past.

    d. Be your own best friend.

    e. Look to the future instead of criticizing or glorifying the past.

    f. Accept criticism and learn from it.

    g. Accept compliments and pat yourself on the back.

Writing your story

Meridyth was a chief surgical nurse I coached a few years ago. She was raising two pre-teen children and handling a demanding and stressful job. When her twenty-year marriage dissolved, she let herself gradually gain almost sixty pounds. She knew it was unhealthy, and that she was headed down the road to diabetes, following in her mother's footsteps. So, when her knees gave out and her doctor told her that she had to lose the weight, she couldn't just say okay and thanks. She denied it, "I'm not that fat, I'm wearing heavy winter clothes." And, deluded herself, "I'm starting a diet next week that will take off the pounds in no time." And, expressed contempt, "My responsibilities with the surgical team force me to work through lunch so I don't have time to go to that expensive natural foods grocery store at noon. Junk food is my only alternative." And, she judged others, "My parents were fat, and I learned all my eating habits from them, and besides, Jeff left me for a twenty-something, so I'm doomed."

When I met her, she was resisting the obvious. In our early conversations, at one time or another, she hid behind all of the following:

✓ Fear of changing and losing part of your identity. "If I lose 40 pounds, my fat friends won't like me anymore."

✓ Anxiety over who you will "have to be" with the new knowledge. "I realize that I am putting myself at risk for having diabetes, just like my mother, if I don't lose the weight, but I can't picture eating salads for the rest of my life."

✓ Guilt for believing something that was counter to what you learned from people you have loved and trusted. "I should have listened to my husband, before my weight got so out of control. He really did have my best interests in mind."

✓ Pride in being right, so you are reluctant to admit you have misunderstood reality. "I am a nurse by training. I should have known that my weight was affecting my health."

✓ Shame about how this information reflects on you. "I am overweight. I have to really look in the mirror and admit it."

✓ Regret over not having understood earlier. "If I had admitted my weight problem a few years ago, I probably could have prevented the knee injury that is causing me so much pain."

✓ Anger at yourself for deceiving yourself. "Why didn't I see what was happening with my weight?"

✓ Embarrassment over past actions. "I shudder to think about what people must think of me as a nurse who is so overweight."

By recognizing that these "excuses" are not valid, she was on her way to accepting the tough answers to the questions that she was asking herself. She forged ahead and wrote her "I AM" statements that included:

✓ I am overweight, but I am on the road to a healthier life.
✓ I am a healthcare professional, and I will live the principles that I teach others.
✓ I am an excellent mother, and plan to dance at my child's wedding.

She accepted the tough truths, formed positive affirmations, used her self-power to make the needed changes, took strong actions, and realized her goals.

The importance of your story

What Meridyth also did was change her story about herself. Her original story about herself was that she was a victim of "fat genes," an unfaithful husband, and a stressful career. Her new story is that she is a healthy, future-oriented mother and healthcare professional. Jim Loehr in his book *The Power of Story* (Loehr, 2008) says that your story *is* your life. If you write your story that you are powerless, a victim, worthless, and unlovable, the reality is that your life probably will track with your story. Not a good place to start. Change your story to one of power, faith, and self-compassion, and your life will change. To start from where you are, write the story that you want for your life. Your story tells you who you are and who you are not. So, what's your story?

EXERCISE IN STARTING FROM WHERE YOU ARE

1. Write ten affirmations that start with I AM. Be honest with yourself, but also be kind and compassionate with yourself. Don't deny your strengths or your weaknesses. Be there for yourself. Accept responsibility for where you are and who you are.
2. Write ten affirmations that start with I AM NOT. They should be descriptive and positive in tone, not negative.
3. For each affirmation, give it a score of 1 to 10, with 10 being "I know this is true" and 1 being "I wish it were true but it is not."
4. Meet with a trusted friend (or two or three friends) and review your affirmations. Ask the friend to grade your affirmations from their point of view. How do they match to your own grades? Talk with the friend about any big differences.
5. Modify your affirmations based on your new perspective.

Conclusion

Roomba® has some pretty amazing software built into its little "brain." It understands its strengths (Boy, can I suck up dirt from your carpet! I will solve your problems!) and its weaknesses (No, I can't clean draperies, so don't put me on a wall). It has a balance between self-esteem and self-assessment. It has a personal story that emphasizes both. Its story is "I AM an outstanding robotic floor vacuum cleaner."

What's your story? How is that story opening doors for you? Start from where you are!

Chapter 2

Commit to your vision, even if you don't know all that it entails

Roomba® has a vision; a healthy living space free of dust, dirt, pet fur, dander, and pollen. It's a challenging, but achievable, vision of my home. Roomba® has a mission; to vacuum each assigned room in an efficient and effective manner. Roomba® has goals; suck up all the dirt today and be ready to do it again tomorrow. And, Roomba® has core values; reliability, effectiveness, and responsiveness. We are all familiar with corporate vision statements, mission descriptions, lists of goals, and core value statements in business. Defining and committing to these same concepts on a personal level is less common, but perhaps even more important. When I put Roomba® on the floor in one of my rooms and press the "clean" button, it jumps into action with energy and enthusiasm, even if it has never been in that room in the past. Roomba® commits to its vision of giving me a healthy home even when it doesn't know what challenges it will face.

Let's pretend that your long-awaited, precious two-week vacation starts today. You pack a bag with a few outfits for different temperatures and weather conditions, drive to the airport, and then randomly get on the first plane that has an available seat. When you arrive at the unknown city, you hop in a cab and ask the driver to take you to an interesting place. After you spend some time at the museum where the cab driver dropped you, a billboard for a movie catches your eye. Late into the evening it's time to find a hotel, so you ask a passerby on the street where a nice hotel is located. For two weeks you follow whatever comes your way. Is this your idea of a perfect vacation? Probably not. Most people dream about their vacations, look at a multitude of brochures, research, compare, schedule flights and hotels far in advance, and make lists of "must do's" to take advantage of every minute.

Memorable vacations don't just happen, they are planned. Most of us live the majority of our lives without plans or goals. Think of what your life could be, if you put that same amount of planning and thought into the other fifty weeks of the year.

A personal vision statement answers the question, "Where am I going?" and gives you a mental image of an achievable and desirable future for yourself. A personal mission statement answers the question, "Who am I?" and is an expression of your values and the criteria by which you will measure everything else in your life. Your personal goals define how you are going to reach your vision. Your core values are the traits or qualities that are the deeply held beliefs and guiding principles that are the basis for how you make decisions.

Writing your personal vision and mission helps you to:

- ✓ Discover your interests, talents and desires.
- ✓ Think deeply about your life, your purpose, and what is really important to you.
- ✓ Clarify and express your deepest values and aspirations.
- ✓ Solidify your values so they become part of you, instead of something you think about occasionally.
- ✓ Define your path so you are motivated, driven, and see the bigger picture.
- ✓ Internalize your values and vision so it is easier to make choices as they arise.
- ✓ Set life priorities and manage life-work balance.
- ✓ Energize your life.
- ✓ Communicate who you are and where you are going.
- ✓ Identify congruence with the vision and mission of your employer, a future employer, your significant other, your family, and your friends.

Living in a situation where there is disharmony between your vision and mission, and the vision and mission of those around you leads to stress and unhappiness.

Your Personal Vision Statement

Your personal vision statement puts into words a clear, concise, and positive image of who you want to be in the future. The clearer and more specifically you describe your vision, the more likely it is that you will be able to embody that vision and achieve the life you want. Think of this as your own definition of success. After you write your personal vision statement, share it with the key people in your life. This will solidify your commitment to the vision, and build a network of support. The difference between a vision and a dream is that a vision has direction, dedication, discipline, and deadlines. The difference between a vision and a hallucination is the number of people who see it.

Some examples of vision statements I have seen are:

- ✓ In five years I want to receive the Entrepreneur of the Year award in my city, with my wife and son standing by my side.
- ✓ In five years I want to be on the first step of my career ladder, with my degree in my pocket and a cool apartment in New York City.
- ✓ In five years I want to be managing a non-profit organization that helps underprivileged children in an urban setting.
- ✓ In five years I want to be happily married with two kids, a dog, and be very active in my church.
- ✓ In five years I want to be the Vice President of supply chain management in my organization, and have a vacation cottage on the lake that I will enjoy very frequently with my wife and two sons.

Your Personal Mission Statement

A mission statement is different from a vision statement because it defines your purpose in life; the "why" in your life. This is what you use to measure everything else in your life.

Some examples of mission statements are:

- ✓ My mission is to be a loving and supportive wife and mother, and leave the world in good shape for my children.
- ✓ My mission is to be a good and loyal friend; a trusted and strong employee, and, a dedicated mother and daughter.
- ✓ My mission is to create a business where employees love to work and clients love the service.
- ✓ My mission is to educate students in the facts and philosophy of life.
- ✓ My mission is to be "a true man" in everything I do.

Your Personal Goals

Your goals are the specific actions you will do to achieve your mission and vision. Well-defined goals give you clarity, direction, motivation and focus. Goals help you to:

- ✓ Make positive changes in your life.
- ✓ Form new habits, or change existing habits.
- ✓ Improve or develop skills, talents, or abilities.
- ✓ Realize an important outcome, and make progress towards your vision.
- ✓ Improve your performance on a task or activity.
- ✓ Focus your energy and efforts towards the desired outcome.
- ✓ Give you a target to aim for.
- ✓ Enhance motivation, persistence, and desire for success.
- ✓ Help you to establish priorities in keeping with the long-term view of what is most important to you.
- ✓ Give you a roadmap to success, allowing for detours and shortcuts.
- ✓ Give you valuable feedback as to whether or not you are making progress.
- ✓ Illustrate the process in life, rather than just the end result, teaching us to live in the moment.

Some examples of goal statements are:

✓ My goal is to finish my MBA degree within three years, and maintain at least a 3.8 GPA.
✓ My goal is to spend at least two Saturdays a month doing something special with my children, with no interruptions from cell phones or emails from the office.
✓ My goal is to have a complete physical in January, and then schedule and follow through the doctor's recommendations the rest of the year.
✓ My goal is to take lessons in pottery in both the spring and fall semester, and never miss a class.
✓ My goal is to complete a succession plan for the key managers in my company by March; then develop and implement the training programs by October.
✓ My goal is to read at least one novel each month, not only for relaxation but in order to expand my learning.

Your Core Values

Core values are those traits or qualities that represent your being. They are the things that are most important to you. Some examples of how core values can be expressed are:

✓ Love – Love for my family and friends is most important to me.
✓ Authenticity – I want to be authentic in everything I do or say.
✓ Fun - I want to have fun in life, and show others that fun is an important component of life.
✓ Learning – I want to be a lifelong learner.
✓ Honesty – Being honest in every interaction is important to me.
✓ Fairness – I will work to be fair, and to encourage fairness.
✓ Beauty – I want to create beauty in the world.

- ✓ Trust – I want to be trusting and trustworthy in everything I do.
- ✓ Ethics – I will act ethically in every aspect of my life, and work to instill ethical values in those around me.
- ✓ Diversity – I embrace cultural diversity, and promote it in my work and personal life.

Reality Check

In order to take stock of your current situation, do this exercise. First, write down a detailed description of what you did yesterday. Describe how you felt when you woke up in the morning, every interaction during the day, who were the key people in your life, and how you felt at the end of the day. Summarize the emotions you felt during the day; happy, sad, contented, uplifted, challenged, bored, stressed, conflicted. Now, describe what your day will look like exactly one year from now. Who will be in your life? What will you be doing? Most important, how will you feel? On a new piece of paper, describe what your day will be like exactly five years from now. Answer the same questions. What will be different? What path will your life be on? Now compare the three days. Is this the trajectory you want in your life? If not, what would you like to be different? What parts of your life do you value? What are you doing to treasure and protect those parts? What relationships are influencing your life, and how will you safeguard them? If your life were to end exactly five years from today, would you be happy with the description of your last day? It's time to think of the rest of your life as if it were your precious vacation time. It's time to envision your life!

Write your personal vision, mission, goals and core values

The next step is to set aside some time to write your own personal vision, mission, goals, and core value statements.

VISION EXERCISE

1. Visualize yourself at the end of your life, content, proud, having achieved everything you wanted to achieve, and done everything you wanted to do. Describe what that looks like, and how that feels.
2. Write what you would like to have on your gravestone in five to seven words.
3. Write down who you want to be in the future, not what you want to have or do, but the full measure of the person you want to be.
4. Capture how you see yourself in your most fulfilling roles in your career, family, community, and spiritual community.
5. Describe your sense of purpose and inspiration.
6. Describe the legacy you want to leave to the next generation.
7. From these thoughts, write a vision for your future that consists of two to three sentences, in a clear, positive description of whom you want to be in the future.
8. Carry this vision with you for a few weeks, reviewing it routinely.
9. Document your vision. Ask yourself if you would be proud to have this vision statement hanging in your office or home. Commit to your personal vision.
10. Share your vision with those who are closest to you. This will help you keep on track, and you can count on them to support you when things are tough. Your energy will be magnified by their support.
11. Review your vision routinely, and make changes so it is a living document that reflects who you are becoming.

MISSION EXERCISE

1. Why is your vision important to you? Why do you want to achieve this?
2. How do you want to be perceived as you journey towards your vision?
3. If you were to write a "marketing tagline" to describe yourself, what would it say?
4. Describe the guiding principles that will direct your actions every day.
5. Select the key principles that will inspire you to reach your vision.
6. Write these key principles and keep them in front of you for a few weeks. Are you living them? Are you implementing them? How should you rewrite them to make them clearer?
7. Would you be proud to have these key principles openly displayed in your office and your home?
8. Would others see that you live by these key principles? If not, why not?

GOAL-SETTING EXERCISE

1. Define personal goals in all of the following domains:
   a. Personal Development – education, personal skills, personal growth.
   b. Health – health and wellbeing, including exercise, fitness, nutrition, rest.
   c. Career – work, and work-related learning and skill development.
   d. Family – relationship with spouse, children, parents, siblings, extended family.
   e. Financial – fiscal responsibility, security, investment wealth.
   f. Recreation – relaxation, hobbies, adventures, vacations.

     g. Friends – relationships with close friends and general acquaintances.

     h. Community – community involvement and service to others, volunteerism, political offices, service on boards, service to alma mater, educational participation.

     i. Spiritual – religion, meditation, self reflection.

     j. Household – type of home environment, geography, home ownership, neighborhood.

2. Each of the goals must be consistent with your mission and vision.

3. For each of the domains, ask yourself, "<u>What</u> do I want to accomplish in this role?"

4. For each of the domains, ask yourself, "<u>Why</u> do I want to accomplish this goal?"

5. Each goal must be "SMART."

    S = specific and significant.

    M = measurable and meaningful.

    A = achievable and action-oriented.

    R = responsible, realistic, and relevant.

    T = timely, with a determined timeframe.

6. For each goal, describe how it uses your strengths, helps to shore up a weakness, takes advantage of an opportunity, and sidesteps a threat.

7. For each goal, work on action plans to reach the goals.

8. List the obstacles that you will face for each goal and plan contingencies, or fall-back positions.

9. List what it will take to reach the goal; time, money, opportunity cost, and effort. Be sure you are willing to give what it takes to reach the goal.

10. List people and networks that you will need to engage in order to reach the goal.

11. Celebrate each time you reach a goal.

CORE VALUE EXERCISE

1. Make a long list of values that are important to you.
2. Select from the list five values that touch your heart and soul. Values that define you.
3. Write a one sentence description of each of the core values.
   Reflect on how you are living in compliance with these core values. What should you change? Where is there a divergence? What can you do to better live in harmony with these values?

PULL IT TOGETHER EXERCISE

1. Review your core values, goals, mission, and vision. Are they consistent and in harmony?
2. If you achieve your goals, will you fulfill your mission and vision?
3. Are your core values reflected in your goals, mission, and vision?
4. Are your actions today in harmony with your core values, goals, mission, and vision? If not, what needs to change?
5. Do your personal core values, goals, mission, and vision mesh with those of your employer? With your current career path? With those of your family? With those of your significant other? If not, what actions do you need to take?
6. Review your core values, goals, mission, and vision routinely, and make path-correcting adjustments so your commitments and reality align.

REALITY CHECK

Check if your vision, mission and core values match with those of your employer

1. Write down what you think your direct supervisor's vision, mission and core values are.
2. Do your supervisor's vision, mission and core values mesh with yours?
3. If someone were to ask the people who report to you what they think your vision, mission and core values are, what would they say?
4. What would you want them to say?
5. In the next six months, what specific steps are you going to take, so if we asked them again, they would say exactly the same as your answer in # 4 above?
6. Commit to taking those steps.

Conclusion

Roomba® has a personal vision, mission, goals, and core values that are unified and consistent. Your challenge is to *actively* direct your life towards the future you want.

Chapter 3

Be ready to take on a new opportunity

Roomba® sits quietly in the corner of the family room, snugged up against the docking station, battery fully charged, waiting for me to tap the "clean" button. With a four note song, a circular spin, and a whirring sound, off it goes. The Roomba® "brain" has algorithms that allow it to determine the size of a room, a pattern for cleaning, and a way to get out of tight jams, even in rooms it has never seen before. It's prepared to take on any challenge or new opportunity, the living room, bedroom, dining room, or the dreaded cat fur-covered family room. Roomba® is always ready!

Have you ever looked at a new product and thought that it was so obvious you should have invented it? Have you ever read a page in a book, and realized that you have no idea what you just read? Have you looked at a clock three times before you actually knew what time it was? Did you ever realize that you can see what you expect to see? Like the time the mustached colleague showed up for work clean shaven and was disappointed you didn't notice. Did you ever notice that some people always seem to be in the right place at the right time?

Some people change paradigms, create new products, identify new markets, and seem to do it all with ease. Well, it's not luck, chance, or dreaming. It's being fully prepared to recognize an opportunity when it presents itself. How can you be one of these "lucky" ones? Become a *mindful expert*.

Expertise is within your control

The *Cambridge Handbook of Expertise and Expert Performance*, published by Cambridge University Press in 2006, is a 900–plus page compilation of contributions from more than 100 leading scientists who have studied expertise and top performance in a wide variety of domains, including surgery, acting, chess, writing, computer programming, ballet, music, aviation, firefighting, and many others (Ericsson, Charness, Feltovich, & Hoffman, 2006). The conclusion: Experts are always made, not born. And, yes, practice does make perfect.

Does this mean that your innate skill and genetic makeup have no impact? No. Our genes and heredity pull us in certain directions and limit us from others. Studies have shown that physical traits, such as height, size, or strength may prevent someone from succeeding in an endeavor, but it does not ensure their success. A college freshman who is five feet five inches tall may not be the first pick for the basketball team but the six feet five inch man will not be successful on the team without developing his skills. Dean Simonton at the University of California at Davis estimates that between 22% and 36% of the differences in creative achievement in the arts and sciences can be explained by heredity. In his book, *Genius 101*, (Simonton, 2009) he discusses how genius is typically in a particular domain, not universal, and is influenced by many factors in addition to genetics, including intellectual stimulation at home during the formative years, early exposure to skills, and interaction with heterogeneous groups. Note that this leaves a lot of expertise and genius that is molded by environmental factors. K. Anders Ericsson from Florida State University summarized his research in a recent article in Harvard Business Review, entitled *The Making of an Expert* (Ericsson, Prietula, & Cokely, *The Making of an Expert*, 2007). He correlates expertise with intensive deliberate practice, devoted teachers or mentors, and enthusiastic family support. Deliberate practice is not just doing the same thing over and over again. It is specific and sustained hard work to do something you can't do now. Lots of work. His research shows that even the most gifted individuals need a minimum of ten years, or 10,000 hours, of intense training before they become true experts in their fields.

Malcolm Gladwell reinforced and expanded these ideas in his book *Outliers* (Gladwell, 2008). He agrees with Ericsson that to become an expert, an investment of over 10,000 hours of effort is needed. But his book also puts success into the context of learning, culture, family history, childhood, geography, chance happenings, and your place in history.

This is where you step in. If only a maximum of 35% of genius is determined by factors beyond your control, that gives you *65%* that is in your control!

To be ready to recognize and take advantage of a new opportunity, you have to have expertise. You are a unique combination of all the factors that the researchers have found to be important, your childhood, your family heritage, personal experiences, culture, values, and genes. Now layer on top of that *deliberate practice* to sharpen your skills.

Deliberate Practice

Practice alone makes you an experienced non-expert. Deliberate practice involves thoughtful, intentional, hard work, incorporating feedback, and getting expert assistance to improve.

Many researchers studied students learning Morse Code in order to understand how we learn and become experts. They chose this system because it was easy to measure speed and accuracy in translating messages from auditory to writing and from writing to auditory. In their classic studies of Morse Code operators, Bryan and Harter (Bryan & Harter, 1897) (1899) concluded that in learning the skill of sending and receiving coded messages, performance would generally reach a plateau, and the students could only improve beyond the plateau by changing learning methodology. They suggested that in learning Morse code, one must learn a hierarchy of habits. First, the students had to learn the symbols for the letters, and then become comfortable with syllables and words and finally with phrase and sentences. To become a full expert, the student had to progress through these stages. Bryan and Harter concluded that a plateau in learning means that the lower-order habits have been mastered, but are not sufficiently automatic to allow the student to put attention on the higher level habits.

F. S. Keller delved into it more deeply (Keller, 1958) in his work. He theorized that the first step in learning Morse Code is to memorize a list of visual dot-dash symbols, one for each letter and digit. The student's first response to an auditory signal, when he/she hears the dot and dash, is to visualize, or internally verbalize, the dot-dash elements of the code. Then, the student uses a sub-vocal articulation of the appropriate character; and, finally the student writes or openly speaks the letter or digit. In every case of reaction to a signal, there is this chain of events, four steps in all, hearing the symbols, visualizing or internally verbalizing the symbols, translating to the letter or character in the brain, and then writing or saying the translated character. In responding to a simple combination of a short and long tone, for example, a student would focus on hearing the dot and dash, then would visualize a dot and a dash, utter sub-vocally the letter "a," and then write the letter down – all within a second or two.

As the student becomes more experienced, several more things happen. Shortcuts happen. For example, the initial visualizing or verbalizing within each chain is replaced by a shortcut response. Instead of reacting to the dot – dash sounds by saying "dot-dash" or seeing the dot and dash, the student may say to himself something like "di-dah;" a muscular approximation to the tonal pattern. With further practice, this step may drop out of the chain completely, so the reaction time is appreciably shortened. With even more practice, each response chain begins to overlap in time with its neighbors, resulting in significant increases in speed.

Tulloss, (Tulloss, 1918) took this one step further and suggested that a Morse code expert may be writing several words or phrases delayed, bringing in the role of memory, patterning, context and anticipatory hearing to the learning process. So, to overcome a learning plateau, the student has to change the method of learning, engaging a wider range of skills.

This is much like learning to drive. In those first few terrifying lessons in a mall parking lot, you are so concerned with how to turn the wheel, how hard to push on the brake, that you can't imagine going on a highway. Many of us actually whispered commands to ourselves. "Brake, brake, brake, signal, turn, stop…" Turn the clock forward 10,000 hours and we can listen to music, talk on the phone, and navigate our way to new places, all at the same time. We have become highly experienced drivers and have formed brain shortcuts to allow ourselves to advance. Are we driving experts? No, not in the way that Formula One or NASCAR drivers are. We are experienced non-experts. We have reached a learning plateau, but for most of us, this is the level that we need and want. What would it take to become an expert, professional driver? Mac Demere is a journalist, who has written for *Motor Trend*, *Popular Mechanics*, edmunds.com, *Kelley Blue Book* and others. He was editorial director of *SportsCar* and *Performance Racing Industry* magazines. He's a driving and tire safety expert and a former race car driver, who competed in the NASCAR Southwest Tour and the Rolex 24 at Daytona. In a recent article (Demere, 2007) he summarized what it takes to be a race car driver: make a huge commitment, expand your mechanical knowledge of cars, volunteer to work on a race team to learn from experts, and practice to improve your technical skills, especially in car control. Then, be willing to give up your time, money, relationships and possibly your life to succeed. He has defined deliberate practice to become a driving expert.

The most interesting part of this theory is that the same process applies to much more difficult learning. Dr. Atul Gawande is a surgeon, writer, and researcher in public health. He practices general and endocrine surgery at Brigham and Women's Hospital in Boston. He is also Associate Professor of Surgery at Harvard Medical School, and Associate Professor in the Department of Health Policy and Management at the Harvard School of Public Health. His research work currently focuses on systems innovations to transform safety and performance in surgery, childbirth, and care of the terminally ill. In his recent article, *Personal Best*, in *The New Yorker*, (Gawande, 2011) he describes how he spent years developing his skills as a surgeon with over 2,000 surgeries, two thirds of those in his specialty of endocrine organ surgery. He measured his patient complication rates against the national averages and saw continual improvements. Until he hit a plateau. Medicine is a fast-evolving science, so physicians have to run to stay in place. But, determined to continue his learning trajectory, Dr. Gawande hired a retired general surgeon and his former teacher as his surgical coach. Dr. Gawande said that after the first surgery observed by his coach, he had more things to consider and work on than he had in the previous five years. As a third-party observer, the coach could see improvements on how the patient was draped with the surgical cloths, the positioning of the lights, the location of the assistants, as well as the position of Dr. Gawande's arms and legs. Dr. Gawande also began watching colleagues to learn from peers. By getting immediate feedback and engaging an expert coach, Dr Gawande is learning through deliberate practice.

Learning and increasing skills stop when we run out of time to put into it, because of other demands on our time, when we lose motivation or interest, or, when we don't know how to improve from where we are. Deliberate practice leads to continued learning and expertise. Deliberate practice is breaking your goal into small pieces that can be practiced, and then increasing the difficulty of the practice session to be outside of your comfort zone. It is a continuing dedication of time, interest, and finding new ways to learn. It may take 10,000 hours of deliberate practice to become an expert violinist, swimmer, tennis champ, programmer, or CEO. But it may take only ten hours of deliberate practice to improve the way you prioritize your daily work, and that improvement in productivity may be a big step towards your ultimate goal.

Recently, I taught an undergraduate-level course in Operations Management in the business school of a liberal arts college near Philadelphia. On the first day of class I asked each student to introduce himself or herself, including what they wanted to be when they grew up. I got some of the usual answers of "I don't want to grow up," and "I don't know yet." But, one young man was clear, positive, and proud. His goal was to be a professional bass fisherman. I was completely unfamiliar with the world of competitive fishing so at first I thought he was kidding. However as the semester went on I got to know him and realized that he was passionate about the sport and was very accomplished. He was a national champion, winning many competitions with very large cash prizes. At one point, I asked him why he was getting a degree in business if his passion was competition fishing. He told me that bass fishing was his passion and his life, so he wanted to be prepared to follow any related path that it took him. He said that he envisioned perhaps having a business providing fishing vacation tours, maybe designing better equipment, or having a retail pro shop. I was impressed. A twenty year old college senior understood using deliberate practice to build the foundation for an exciting career in the field of his passion.

In the early years of my career, I was a research scientist in Biochemistry. Scientific methodology was second nature to me. Form a hypothesis, design a controlled experiment with only one variable, run the experiment, analyze the data, compare to the hypothesis, refine the hypothesis, repeat. That's how scientific discoveries are made, rarely through a stroke of genius, and usually by repeating the above process hundreds of times. This recipe for deliberate practice works in almost any field.

Several years ago, I was coaching Joe, a brilliant scientist who was working to develop novel compounds for pharmaceutical uses. He had just been promoted to manage a diverse team and was failing miserably in his new responsibilities; not an unusual story. The scientist, now manager, was struggling with his new role. What was unusual was that he was determined to become expert in leading a team. He set about reading every book he could get his hands on. He asked colleagues who they thought was an excellent manager. He watched those managers, first from a distance, then approached two and asked for feedback on his own style. The hardest step was when he sat down with each of his direct reports and asked for critique and suggestions. When he demonstrated his openness to hear the worst without repercussions, he got very valuable information. He formed a hypothesis that his staff felt that he was not clearly communicating his expectations to them, so they felt that they were always guessing what he wanted. He decided to try an experiment. He told his staff that whenever they felt that he was not communicating clearly they should use the word "jabberwocky." If he was not sure that he was clear, he would ask if he was being "a jabberwocky." "Jabberwocky" could be a noun, verb, adjective, or adverb. "You jabberwockied that memo." "Would you please unjabberwocky that for me?" By using a funny, unusual word, he got immediate feedback, but the staff was comfortable and open with him. He kept notes on how many times he was "a jabberwocky," and reflected on what he had said or done to deserve the feedback. After a few months, the word almost completely disappeared from the staff vocabulary.

Joe used deliberate practice to become a better manager. He was committed to becoming a skilled manager, and took a first step to achieve his goal. He pushed himself past his comfort zone and asked for critical feedback. He recognized that he had a limitation, sought feedback, tested a new approach, and used the results to continue to improve. By applying deliberate practice to a weakness, he saw immediate positive results.

Anne, on the other hand, took a completely different, but equally effective, approach to deliberate practice. When she joined the human resources department in a large company, she was assigned to the team responsible for administering health care benefits. The other team members had been in the department for several years and were happy to bring her up to speed and share the work load. Anne realized that her colleagues were extremely experienced in their jobs, but had not looked beyond the edges of their desks. They were experienced non-experts. She began to notice patterns in the health care claims, and read all the information sent by the insurance companies. She asked her boss if the company had considered focusing on keeping the employees healthy instead of treating their illnesses. He challenged her to expand on her idea. Like a dog with a bone, she pursued the idea until she had a concept that she could bring to her boss. She continued to challenge herself, and challenge the ingrained ideas at the company. She eventually changed the culture of the organization to focus on improving wellness, reducing labor costs, insurance costs, and increasing the morale of the workforce. She used deliberate practice to become a race car driver in her field.

A few weeks ago, the ten year old son of a friend had convinced me (using that soulful look that only a ten year old boy can do) to buy six tickets for the fundraiser for his boy scout troop. For twenty dollars a ticket, they boasted six "famous" comedians, including two "headliners" and four "up and coming" comedians for a night of laughs and friendship in the middle school auditorium. We convinced two other good-spirited couples to join us on a cold winter night by bribing them with a home-cooked meal. At the intermission of what turned out to be a fun evening, I saw a friend across the auditorium. He did not live in our town so I asked why he chose to support Troop 848. He and I served on a board of directors together and he was also the Congressman from our district. He told me that he sought out comedy performances whenever he could. He pointed out that public speaking was critical to success in his career in politics. He said that a successful comedian makes the audience relaxed, so they are receptive and focus on listening to the stories and jokes. The audience becomes supportive and encouraging. They end up liking the comedian as well as the jokes. When an unskilled comedian is on the stage, the audience becomes tense and they focus on the comedian, not the stories. They wiggle in their seats with discomfort and almost pain. They dislike the comedian for making them uncomfortable. My friend said that he came to the event, not to laugh, but to watch for the subtle differences between a skilled comedian and a novice. He was using this approach as a deliberate practice to improve his own public speaking skills so he could better connect with his audiences and they would focus on his message. Sometimes the expert mentor and coach comes from a very different field.

The key elements of deliberate practice are:

- ✓ Work to improve your expertise, not just through repetition, but through unique, deliberate exercises. Practice smarter, not just harder.
- ✓ Follow your passion, because if you are not passionate about what you are doing, you will give up, get bored or lose interest. Feed your passion and stay motivated.
- ✓ Look for immediate feedback, so you know whether you are going in the right direction. Feedback comes in many forms, and sometimes it's hard or painful to hear. But without feedback to correct your trajectory, you could be way out in left field before you know it.
- ✓ Incorporate the feedback to make course corrections along the way.
- ✓ Think deliberately. Try to extend the reach of your learning to new areas and shore up your weak areas. Push yourself beyond your comfort zone.

- ✓ Set specific learning goals, not result goals, *learning goals*. Focus on techniques, not outcomes; processes, not results.
- ✓ Find an expert coach or mentor to encourage and direct your learning, and, most important, to give you that painful feedback. Emulate the experts around you.
- ✓ Think two levels up. What skills will you need to learn now to be ready for two levels up?
- ✓ Practice consistently. There is no magic bullet that will make it easier, so stop searching for it. There are no shortcuts. This is hard work.

As with anything, there are risks to becoming an expert.

- ✓ Overconfidence in one's own ability.
- ✓ Seeing situations only from one's own perspective, and not looking for new input.
- ✓ Making decisions without thinking.
- ✓ Missing the details.
- ✓ Judging people who may not be at your level, and assuming that they have nothing to contribute.
- ✓ Focusing only on goals, not on the process.
- ✓ Doing things the same way, because that's what you have always done.

Mindful Expert

Being an expert is great. But, how can you avoid the pitfalls of expertise? And, is that enough to see and take advantage of a new opportunity? To be creative? I think not. Let's add one more layer. Mindfulness.

Mindfulness is active and open full attention to the present. It is observing, not judging; being in the present, and being open to new information. Since the 1970s, the term has been used to describe a wide range of activities, from Zen Buddhism, meditation, and stress reduction methodologies, to just being aware of what's going on around you. Groundbreaking work in this area, particularly in the application of mindfulness to health and learning was done by Ellen J. Langer (Langer, 1989) (Langer, 1997) (Langer, 2009)

A Mindful Expert is:

- ✓ Being ready for a new solution to an old problem.
- ✓ Recognizing change as it's happening.
- ✓ Recognizing novelty or newness.
- ✓ Seeing that sometimes one plus one can equal three.

A Mindful Expert is not:

- ✓ Questioning for the sake of questioning.
- ✓ Getting lost in the details.
- ✓ Experiencing paralysis by analysis.
- ✓ Nitpicking.

The opposite of being mindful is to be mindless. Mindlessness looks a lot like the pitfalls of expertise. Mindlessness is:

- ✓ Using yesterday's solutions to today's problems.
- ✓ Assuming tomorrow will be just like today.
- ✓ Making biased decisions.
- ✓ Seeing what you expect to see.

Let's go back to the driving example. I'm not a race car driver, but I'm a competent street driver (although, my husband may disagree with this characterization). And, I did find myself falling into the mindless pitfall of expertise recently. My car is a 2002 Audi, small, nimble, and sporty. Recently, when my car was at the dealer for inspection, my husband offered me his 2012 Jeep Grand Cherokee for my commute to work. Everything about it is different, roomier, much bigger, and it still had that new car smell. After work I was kicking myself because there on the windshield was a parking ticket, with a double violation no less. I had parked in my "usual" spot, for faculty parking with window sticker permits only and in the "economy car" space. I had mindlessly parked my husband's SUV in the usual spot for small cars and without transferring my parking sticker to the windshield. I was doing what I always did.

The following picture (and many other similar brain-teasers) recently made the rounds on the internet and Facebook.

CAN YOU FIND THE THE MISTAKE?

1 2 3 4 5 6 7 8 9 10 11 12 13 14 15

I showed this to several friends. They all looked at it for several minutes, gave me that quizzical look, and eventually laughed. I showed it to four children, ages 9 to 11, and they all saw the mistake immediately. The adults are "expert" readers so they did not focus on the process of reading. It is a clear example of seeing what we expect to see. The children were mindful readers, still curious and open about the process. They immediately saw that the word "the" was repeated.

Another way that mindlessness creeps into our lives and prevents us from recognizing opportunities is when we make assumptions based on the context or surroundings. For example, if you were walking through the jewelry department in a major discount store, and saw an elaborate sparkling necklace, you would assume that it was made of zirconium, not real gems. However, place that same necklace in the window of Tiffany's and you would immediately assume high quality diamonds and 18 carat gold. The context of the necklace would influence your assumptions about it.

An interesting experiment was done in 2007, and reported in the *Washington Post* by Pulitzer Prize winner, Gene Weingarten

(Weingarten, 2007). A youngish, white man, wearing jeans, T-shirt, and a baseball cap stood against a wall in the L'Enfant Plaza metro station in Washington DC during rush hour, with an open violin case on the floor in front of him, seeded with a few dollars and coins, playing a violin. It wasn't just any young man. It was Joshua Bell, one of the most distinguished musicians in the world. And, he wasn't playing just any violin. It was a Gibson ex Huberman, handcrafted in 1713 by Antonio Stradivari, valued at over $3.5 million. And, he wasn't playing show tunes. He played some of the most difficult and intricate music written, including the Chaconne from J.S. Bach's Partita No 2 in D minor. The *Washington Post* staff watched the reaction of the 1,097 people who walked past the violinist. At the set up of the experiment, the *Post* editors were concerned about crowd control. Well, they didn't have to worry. During the forty-five minute concert, only a small handful of people stopped and listened. Most hurried on their way, and when later interviewed, did not even remember the violinist. Throughout the experiment, he got $32.17, and was recognized by only one person. There was no ethnic or demographic pattern to the people who stopped to listen or threw him some money. But, every single time a child walked past, he or she tried to stop and watch. And, every time, a parent pulled the child away. The experiment was to see if people would recognize beauty or talent in an unexpected context. The answer was no.

Applying mindfulness to those areas we want to develop with high levels of expertise allows us to see new opportunities and enhance creativity; to see the unexpected.

Early in my career, I worked for Fortune 100 companies, and business travel was a big part of my weekly routine. I became adept at finding inexpensive flights, navigating through airports, and eating alone in small restaurants in distant cities. I spent a lot of time in hotel rooms. So did Shawn Seipler. In 2008, he was a highly-paid global sales executive for an e-commerce business, married, and had four children. He also spent three or four nights a week in hotel rooms all over the world. The difference is that he was mindful of his surroundings and the workings of the hospitality industry so he asked an important question. What happens to those little bars of soap and little shampoos when I check out? He found out that if the guest did not take the half-used products home, they were thrown out. Over one million bars of soap ended up in landfills every year. So, Seipler decided to investigate whether these bars of soap could be recycled. His research led him to statistics that millions of children all over the world did not have access to soap. One study showed that the top two killers of children younger than five years old, acute respiratory illness and diarrheal disease, could be cut by sixty percent if the children had soap to wash their hands. Seipler and his friend, Paul Till, formed a non-profit organization, Clean the World, (www.cleantheworld.org, 2012) in February 2009, using their savings and retirement funds. After great personal and business challenges, the organization took off, and in less than three years provided over nine and a half million bars of recycled soap in forty five countries, including the United States. These mindful visionaries saw, not a small bar of disposable soap, but a way to improve the lives of millions.

Our brains are inundated with so much information every day that we need to create categories in order to organize and prioritize the information and to function efficiently. However, sometimes those categories prevent us from seeing opportunities. We categorize people into groups or classes, objects into functions, and emotions into good or bad. No one can forget President Ronald Reagan's brilliant change of category during the Oct 21, 1984 Presidential debate with Walter Mondale when he quipped "I want you to know that I will not make age an issue of this campaign. I am not going to exploit, for political purposes, my opponent's youth and inexperience." It is this same categorization that prevents us from recognizing new ideas in the workplace if they are brought forward by summer interns, by the secretary, or by the almost-retired middle manager. By applying mindfulness, we can see beyond those categories and see new opportunities.

I had a very mindful employee who, with a simple change, improved the efficiency and reduced costs in my business. My company did analytical testing, primarily in the environmental field, testing drinking water and waste water. We tested hundreds of samples each day for a wide variety of contaminants. For each test, the lab technician had to pour out a small amount of the sample into a beaker and process the sample for the contaminant of interest, for example, nitrate, ammonia, lead, phosphorus, or copper. This required hundreds of small glass beakers to be available for use, then washed, dried and re-shelved each day. No matter how many beakers we bought, there were never enough, and the availability of clean beakers became a bottleneck in the operation. One very mindful chemist, Mary, solved the problem. She said that one morning she was brushing her teeth and used a small, plastic, disposable cup for water to rinse her mouth. A light bulb went off over her head and she asked herself if these cups could be used as disposable beakers. To test her idea, she bought a bag of 150 cups for $0.89 and took them to the lab. She tested them for contaminants that might come out of the plastic into the sample and affect the results by giving a falsely high result. She tested to see if they would absorb anything from the sample giving a falsely low answer. And finally she tested to see if they would interfere with the test method. When all of the experiments gave acceptable results, she brought the idea to me. We immediately implemented the idea, resulting in dramatic cost savings and streamlining of processes. Mary saw the disposable bathroom cup in a different context and "invented" the disposable lab beaker. She applied mindfulness to solve a work problem that everyone else accepted as the way it is.

My personal journey to increase mindfulness took a giant leap forward when I took painting lessons. I had been running my business for about fifteen years and, as I jokingly told people, I work only half days. My work day was from 7:00 am to 7:00 pm every day. That's only twelve out of twenty four hours, so it was exactly half of a day. I realized that I needed a hobby or some distraction, so I signed up for a class in watercolor painting. During college, I did not take any courses in art because I was a science major and to my uneducated brain, art had no relation to science. So, it was a leap for me to walk into an art class with students ranging from amateurs to semi-professionals. It took almost an entire semester before a fellow student looked at my rough painting of a barn door and said that it was the first time she recognized what I was trying to paint. Embarrassing? Humbling? Challenging? Interesting? Exciting? Creative? Yes, to all of them. Most important, I began to look at the world differently. The sky was no longer blue. It was a mixture of cerulean, azure, and a touch of alizarin. A tree held over fifteen different colors! A pumpkin had the roundness and fullness that represented an entire season of the year. Everything around me took on beauty and meaning.

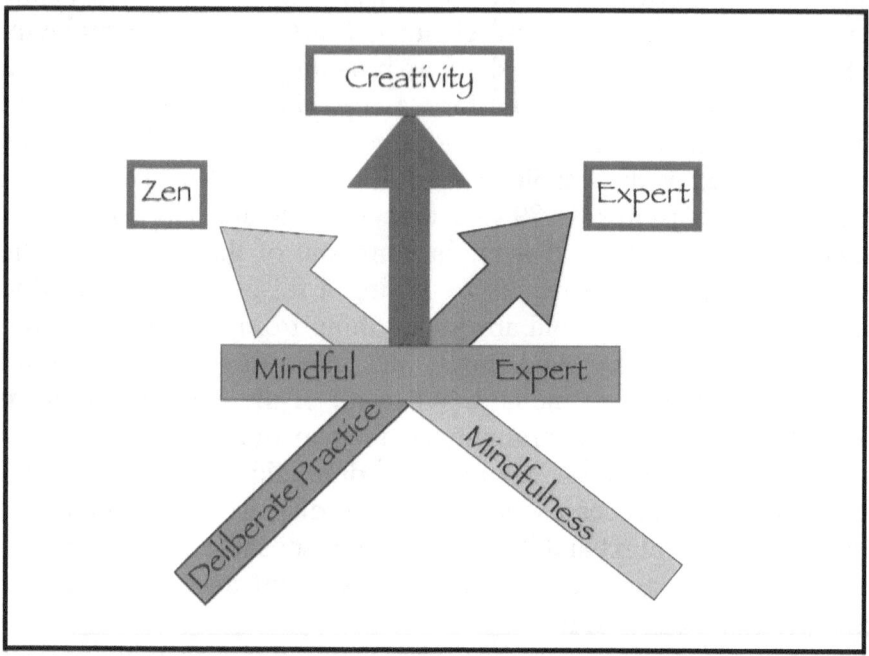

Just like becoming an expert through deliberate practice, becoming mindful requires deliberate, conscious effort. And practice. Creativity, and recognizing the unexpected opportunity, comes from building expertise through deliberate practice and overlaying that with mindfulness.

EXERCISES IN DELIBERATE PRACTICE

1. Read a book published before 1900 and find three ideas that you can use in your business today.
2. Read the biography of someone who is not known in popular culture.
3. Identify one skill you would like to improve, and find someone who is excellent at that skill. Study their technique, and implement at least one thing you learned.
4. Read every story in one issue of *The Wall Street Journal* and describe three trends that you identified.

EXERCISES IN MINDFULNESS

1. Practice listening techniques. If you are an interrupter, count to three before you respond to something that is said to you.
2. Take a class in photography, painting, pottery, or any creative art. It will allow you to see the world through new eyes.
3. Read a random story in a newspaper, and then write down a business idea that would fulfill the needs or wants reflected in the story. Do this every day, and you will find opportunities everywhere.
4. Walk through a kitchen store and find every item that could be used purposefully in your office.
5. Pretend you are describing an experience to someone who does not have the ability to have the same experience. Describe eating ice cream to someone who cannot eat. Describe a rainbow to a blind individual. Describe your favorite song to a deaf person. Describe dancing to a paraplegic.

Conclusion

So, Roomba® sits in the corner of the room, waiting to spring into action. It's an expert in cleaning, and continues to hone its skills every time it's called into action. It's mindful of new situations, not judging, openly curious of the dimensions and parameters of each new room. It's ready to take on a new opportunity.

Chapter 4

When you hit a wall, change direction, but never give up

Press the "clean" button on Roomba's® panel, and it will zoom across the room until it hits an object. Then, it will, after only the slightest hesitation, turn and head in a new direction with as much energy and enthusiasm as before it hit the wall. Roomba® is resilient.

Resilience is the ability to persevere and thrive after an obstacle, a misfortune, stress, or change. Earvin "Magic" Johnson Jr. was a National Basketball League championship player with the Los Angeles Lakers until he abruptly retired in 1991 with the announcement that he had contracted HIV. Since that time, his work to promote prevention, treatment, and a cure for HIV/AIDS has had a greater impact on the world than his years on the court. Candy Lightner founded Mothers Against Drunk Driving (MADD) after her 13 year-old daughter was killed by a drunk driver. She turned a personal tragedy into a way to bring attention to a growing problem.

About two years ago, I met an entrepreneur who was looking for investors in his second business. When I asked about his background and his first business, he told me a most amazing story. He was a senior executive in a pharmaceutical company in New Jersey, on a fast track to a vice president position, happily married, with one daughter. Then, the unimaginable happened. He was in a car accident, hit by a tractor-trailer driven by an over-tired truck driver. His injuries were so severe that the doctors thought he might not live. After four months in a hospital, he was told he would never walk again. He lost his job, and his health insurance along with it. Medical bills kept piling up. His wife left him, giving him full custody of his teenage daughter. His bones were crushed but his spirit was not. As his recovery proceeded slowly but surely, with over twenty surgeries, he progressed from wheelchair, to walker, to crutches, to canes and finally walking independently. Along the way, he noticed that many of the assistive devices for the disabled were heavy, clumsy, and hard to use. He also saw that there was a market for assistive devices that were needed only for short term recoveries. For example, some patients needed a walker for only a few weeks after a surgery. He developed and patented a line of lightweight walkers, canes, and crutches that were inexpensive, colorful, and easy to use. He built the business to a significant size before selling it to a major manufacturer. He hit a wall (literally and figuratively) but his resilience allowed him to not only recover, but to seize a new opportunity.

Recently, I invited a woman entrepreneur to speak to a class I was teaching, to give them a "reality check" on what life is like as a small business owner. With light-hearted laughs and broad sweeps of her hands she told stories of customers not paying bills, company vehicles in accidents, employees stealing money and equipment, employee turnover, and working long hours, every weekend, including every holiday.

When one of the wide-eyed students asked if she ever got discouraged, she admitted that every day in those twelve years she got discouraged, then something great happened and she bounced right back. She ended by telling the students she did not regret one moment of running the business, and would do it all over again. Entrepreneurs have to live and breathe resilience.

These are dramatic examples. But we all hit a wall at some time. Some harder than others. Some more often than others. It could be the loss of a job, loss of a loved one, an injury, disease, or illness, loss of a dream, finding out that something you want is not available to you, having to relocate, surviving a natural disaster, becoming a victim of an economic downturn, being forced into bankruptcy, closing your business, or discovering that a project you are working on failed.

When one hits a wall, there are distinct stages:

1. Shock – the "how could this happen to me?" stage.
2. Disbelief or denial – maybe it's not as bad as they say.

3. Anger or resentment – Why me? What did I do to deserve this? I think I'll sue.
4. Acceptance – I guess it's real.
5. Depression – It's over. Life will never be the same. I give up.
6. Glimmer of light – One step forward.
7. Recovery – I can get back to where I was before. It'll be like it never happened.
8. Seizing the Opportunity – I will be better than before. I have a chance to redefine myself and build on what happened.

We all know people who get stuck in Steps 3, 4 or 5, and maybe some who make it to Steps 6 or 7. Resilience is the ability to get to Step 8. You can be resilient, and it opens up new worlds for you.

You've probably heard of Post Traumatic Stress Disorder, or PTSD. But, the flip side of PTSD is called Post Traumatic Growth or PTG. Post Traumatic Growth is a positive change experienced as a result of the struggle with a major life crisis or a traumatic event. Research in this field was pioneered by University of North Carolina, Charlotte, Professors Richard G. Tedeschi and Lawrence G. Calhoun (Tedeschi & Calhoun, 2004). They have determined that PTG tends to occur in five domains: when a traumatic event opens up a new opportunity, possibility, or life path; a change in relationships with others, such as closer relationships with a specific person or class of people (e.g. others who have cancer); increased sense of one's own strength; greater appreciation for life in general; and deepening of their spiritual life or belief system. Individuals who have demonstrated Post Traumatic Growth have made statements such as:

✓ Things that seemed important before are now insignificant.
✓ I never felt this close to my husband.
✓ I recognize that I am vulnerable, but I feel so strong.
✓ I now understand what others have gone through.
✓ I feel that God helped me through this, because I could not have done it alone.

PTG is a complex phenomenon that can't be described simply as a coping mechanism or a psychological adjustment to the new reality. Tedeschi and Calhoun suggest that it is an iterative process that is likely to involve a powerful combination of emotional relief and a desire to understand the paradox of the tragedy that happened. They propose that the life events that are most likely to result in growth are those that challenge the individual's fundamental assumptions about the world, including assumptions that the world is predictable and controllable, that one is safe and secure, and that others are benevolent and can be trusted.

There are walls everywhere. Here is what to do when you hit a wall:

1. Recognize that you hit a wall. Give yourself some time and get help to get through Stages 1 to 5. You don't have to go through it alone. Talk with those you trust. Reach out for resources to help. The first steps of resilience are similar to the stages in grief. Recognize that you need the time to come through these stages, but set a time limit for yourself. The "deadline" should be reasonable but not too generous. Then stop. Done. Don't wallow in it. Make the decision to move on.

2. Look at the situation with mindfulness. Replay the experience in your mind from the perspective of an outsider, as if you were watching a made for TV movie. Don't judge what happened. Don't find fault or assign blame. It is what it is. Write a story of what happened in a notebook or journal.

3. Decide that you won't let this experience define you. In 2010, I attended the grand opening of a complex of apartments that were designed specifically for handicapped individuals. The project was a life-long dream for Alice. As a result of a degenerative disease, she was a quadriplegic with the use of only three fingers on her left hand. I was amazed at what she had overcome and what she had accomplished in this project. She opened her presentation with the words

"Never let one little thing prevent you from being fabulous." Decide that you will be fabulous.

4. Identify one small, achievable step that will take you into the new direction. Commit to that step and put all your effort into succeeding.
5. Relish your success, then take the next small, achievable step.
6. Formulate a plan. Continue to look forward and take one step at a time.
7. Rejoice in your success.

EXERCISES TO INCREASE YOUR RESILIENCE

1. Build your network of support, especially with people you can count on when things get difficult.
2. Develop your sense of humor. Exercise it like a muscle. Watch skilled comedians, and practice finding humor in every day events. Each day, try to tell a story about an event from the previous day in a funny way, pretending you are on stage at a comedy club. The laughs you get will be a huge reward.
3. Play "what if" games in order to anticipate what could go wrong.
4. Admit that "Sh*&#t Happens," so be on alert for the early signs of change.
5. Be there as a support person for someone else. Witnessing the challenges and successes of others sets an example for you.
6. Volunteer to help in a charity or non-profit to help others. Nothing helps your resilience more than helping someone with bigger challenges. Your mountains become molehills.
7. Practice positivity. Be realistically optimistic.
8. Be flexible and open-minded to new solutions.
9. Look for opportunities for self-discovery. On a routine basis (maybe every day) write down what you have learned about yourself from the experiences of the day.
10. Take care of yourself, physically, mentally, and emotionally.
11. Learn from your past. Look at the successes and failures

you have experienced. Look for patterns. What are your core strengths? What has been a weakness that has gotten in your way?

12. Have a clear vision of what you want to achieve in your life and in your career. When you face a challenge or change, you can fall back on that vision to get you back on track.

13. Engage with change. Change is inevitable, constant, and unpredictable. You will not be able to avoid it, so embrace it and see it as an opportunity.

14. Uncertainty is the only thing that is certain in life. Nothing is predictable, so don't be surprised if you can't predict the future accurately.

15. Have contingency plans for important events in your life and your work. Practice contingency planning in small ways first. For example, find alternate routes to a usual destination or inclement weather planning, until it becomes a habit. Evolve the habit so that contingency planning becomes part of all of your primary plans.

16. Think long-term and plan for the ultimate outcomes. Actively plan for your retirement, write or update your will and power of attorney documents, set up college funds for your children, discuss long-term care with your parents. These may be difficult tasks to take on, but they are necessary, and will allow you to react quickly and confidently when changes occur.

Conclusion

After hitting a wall, Roomba® speeds off in a new direction with optimism, determination and resilience. It doesn't let the wall get in the way of being fabulous. *You* have no reason not to be fabulous !!

Chapter 5

If the wheels get gummed up, progress stops

The first week I owned Roomba®, I admit I probably overworked it. I carried it from room to room and watched it pick up dirt I was embarrassed to admit that I owned. Finally, I had pushed it too far. It stopped dead in its tracks in the middle of the guest bedroom and would not move when I pushed the "clean" button. I rushed it back to the docking station. No, that was not the problem. I pushed the "status" button, and an encouraging voice instructed me to "clean Roomba's® brushes and wheels." The wheels were gummed up, and progress stopped.

Nothing gums up the wheels of progress like worry. Worry is when we tell ourselves that something bad will happen in the future, but we experience the negative emotions now. It is repeatedly putting yourself through something that didn't even happen and probably won't.

This is very different from fear. Fear is our response to a clear and present danger. Fear is good, because it protects us from an imminent threat. It is the evolutionary reaction based in the amygdala portion of the brain, typically with the "fight or flight" response, that preserves our safety. Fear is the reaction one has when coming across a big black snake on the walking path in the woods.

Worry is the thought process that generates the feelings and emotions that we associate with feeling anxious, that can paralyze us into inaction. Worry stifles growth and creativity. It's looking at every stick in the path hoping it's not a snake in disguise. Too often, we justify our worries by pretending it's justified fear. Fear of flying, fear of public speaking, fear of failure, fear of commitment, are examples of emotions that can hold us back from living a full and complete life and having a rewarding career. Everyone has anxiety, worries, and fears. If they are severely debilitating, seek professional help. But, for many people, it's just gumming up the wheels.

Worry can be productive or unproductive. Productive worry is concern for a realistic problem that is solvable and inspires us to take appropriate actions. It puts us on alert and helps us plan for contingencies. Worry about having a healthy retirement causes us to invest in our 401K funds. Worry about our health helps us to eat well and exercise properly.

Unproductive worry focuses on unlikely events, and generates no clear course of action. It results in the negative chatter voice inside our heads that prevents us from moving forward. Instead of useful action, unproductive worry can cause compulsive behaviors, avoidance, procrastination, tension, fatigue, insomnia, or withdrawal. At times we can also have completely abstract, unproductive, overwhelming worry that is not focused on a particular issue. I call it a "worry tummy ache." It is the generalized discomfort with uncertainty or worry about what will happen in the future. It is the mental chatter, the constant commentator providing an overdose of negative thoughts and judgments that is particularly paralyzing.

My early life could be described as "sheltered." Because my family was poor, we never went on vacations and did not have a car, so my travel experiences were limited. My first trip outside of Pennsylvania was at the ripe old age of 22, and it was a day trip to the New Jersey shore. Then, about three months into my first job in a Fortune 100 company, my boss assigned me to visit a supplier outside of Boston and negotiate the purchase of a key raw material. I had never traveled alone, rented a car, driven in a city, or been on an airplane! My worry was a huge fuzzy monster that consumed my every thought. I "knew" that I would get hopelessly lost, miss my flights, cause an accident on the interstate, miss my meeting then get fired from my job. The little voice in my head told me that I was not competent and a coward, and moreover I didn't deserve this cool job. My first reaction was to feign a serious illness or family emergency but quickly realized that my plan would, at best, only postpone the inevitable, and, at worst, maybe tempt fate. So I decided to "put on my big girl clothes" and get it done. I wrote down all of the steps in the trip: house to Philadelphia airport parking lot, parking lot to gate, flight to Boston, airport to rental car office, drive to supplier's office, and then the reverse steps. I wrote down everything that I needed to do in order to successfully make it through each step, had a backup plan for the key steps (okay, I also had a backup plan for the backup plan), and convinced myself that each step was not so bad. I had a detailed map to get me from the airport to the supplier's facility (yes, a paper map, since this was before cars had GPS systems), and I studied the map until it was a shredded piece of paper. When the mental preparation for the trip was done, I had the brain power and focus to think about what I wanted to accomplish during the meeting. I made it. I survived. None of the imagined bad things happened. I succeeded in setting up a long-term supply relationship. I kept the folded map in my coat pocket for over five years. I would routinely touch it to remind myself that I won't let worry hold me back.

In retrospect, I see that my wheels were really gummed up. My worries about the mechanics of the trip were preventing me from embarking on a challenging and important part of my job. I also recognized that my worries were preventing me from focusing on the important part of the assignment, the negotiation of the deal. I didn't realize it at the time, but what I did was to convert unproductive worry into productive worry. The unproductive worry focused on unlikely events in the future that I could not influence. By breaking down the worry into manageable chunks, I analyzed what could go wrong, made a contingency plan, and took useful actions. The unproductive worry paralyzed me. The productive worry enabled me to successfully negotiate a supply contract. Big difference!

One of my clients, Rickey, an entrepreneur who founded a medical device business, described his worries as so all-encompassing that he hadn't slept through the night in over two years. "I'm afraid that I won't get FDA approval on time, that my investors will back out, that I'll get a huge contract with a large pharmaceutical firm and I won't be able to fulfill it, that I won't get the contract with the large pharmaceutical firm and will struggle with sales, that my key employees will give up, that my wife will leave me, that I'll go bankrupt…" and it went on and on. His worries were affecting his health and ability to effectively run his promising business. The only way to get back on track was to get rid of useless worry and make an action plan. For the first week, he kept a detailed log of all of his worries, how scary the outcome would be, how likely the outcome that he feared, and how that worry was affecting him and his business. In the second week, he prioritized the worries, selected the top three and worked through the following decision tree with each one. He saw immediate results and continued to use the tool in order to effectively use his productive worry and keep his unproductive, non-specific worries under control.

Rickey also realized that to be an entrepreneur is to step into an unpredictable world where he was creating his own future. His unproductive, non-specific worries were causing him to question his abilities, and filled him with self-doubt. The more he tried to plan the future of the business and control the direction of the company, the more elusive the vision became. In order to harness his discomfort with uncertainty he needed to address it head-on. The more unpredictable the future seemed to him, the more he worried. The more he worried about the future, the more he was stuck. When he tried to get unstuck, he had habitual thought, action, and speech patterns that escalated his discomfort and made him even more stuck. He needed to break the cycle. He needed to get his "wheels" ungummed.

The first step was to identify the habits that reinforced his non-specific worry. He remembered that his wife always knew when he was worried, because he would chew on the left side of his lower lip. He used this physical signal to make himself aware that worry was on its way. When he caught himself chewing on his lip, he used this signal to immediately stop the flow of thoughts and ask if the incoming worry could be changed into a productive worry with an immediate action plan. If the answer was no, then he used the mental image of putting it on a shelf. If it was yes, then he took action. Every time he stopped the worry before his lip started to hurt, he congratulated himself and gave himself a pat on the back. This visualization allowed him to gain control over his non-specific worry and accept, almost enjoy, the challenges of the unpredictable future of his entrepreneurial venture. He also began to investigate meditation as a way to develop relaxing resiliency. After reading *Comfortable With Uncertainty*, by Pema Chodron (Chodron, 2002), he hung one of her quotes on the wall in his office. It read "You are the sky. The rest is just the weather." He gradually regained confidence in his own ability to analyze, resolve, and overcome challenges as they came his way.

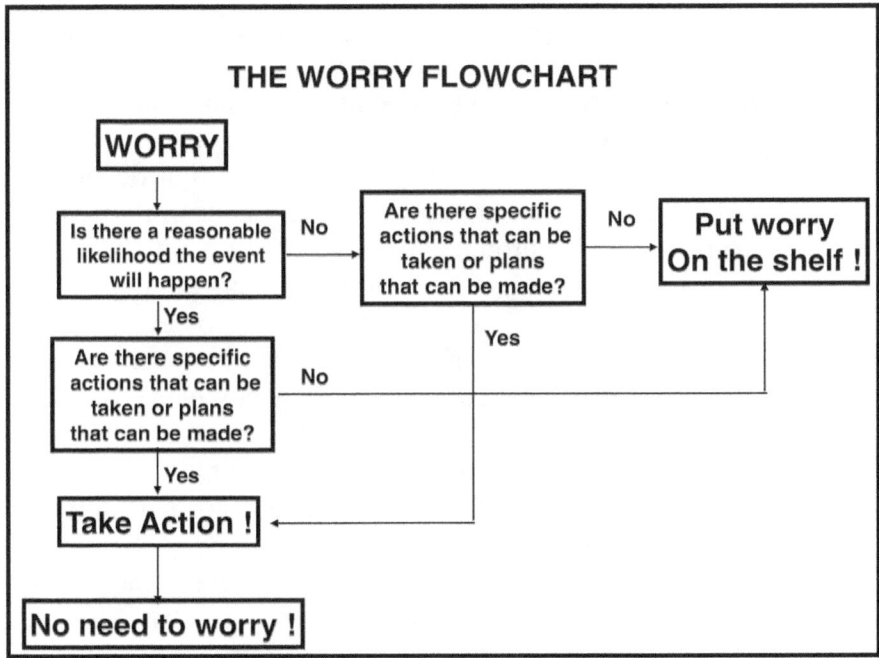

In order to get your wheels unstuck, first analyze your worries and decide whether they are productive or unproductive. And, if unproductive, are they generalized discomfort with an uncertain future, or related to a specific future concern?

> ✓ *Productive worry – Define, refine, and take appropriate actions.* This type of worry can help you achieve your goals if you use it properly. These worries make you aware of real risks, and encourage you to take action. For example, you may be worried that your company will have cutbacks after losing a major customer. Your concern may be justified if the

lost customer cannot be quickly replaced with a new account, so having an updated resume would be an appropriate action.

✓ *Unproductive, specific worry – Analyze, redefine into a productive worry, then take action.* An unproductive, specific worry is when we are concerned about an unlikely event in the future that will have a negative impact. We can distinguish this from a productive worry because the likelihood that the negative event will actually happen is very remote, and there are no obvious actions we can take. For example, you may be worried that the cost of raw materials for your product will increase significantly next year if it is an abnormally cold winter in Florida. This worry is unproductive because you can't change the weather and the likelihood of having an abnormally cold winter is very remote. However, you can redefine it to be a productive worry, such as a concern that you should have contingency plans for all raw materials, and take actions such as negotiating a long-term contract, finding alternate sources in other locations, or finding ways to reduce the costs of other raw materials.

✓ *Unproductive, non-specific worry – Recognize that you are not able to control an uncertain future.* Many of our actions are intended to make our futures more predictable and less risky. But the future is uncertain, and nothing we do will change that. As an example, an unproductive, non-specific worry would be a concern that if you accept the new job offer, you will be stepping into an unknown future, the new company may not like you, and you may be fired. But, you know you are qualified for the job and you will give 120% effort, so the worry is general, unfounded, unlikely, and leads to no new actions. Some approaches to minimizing unproductive, non-specific worry are:

✓ Be curious about the future.
✓ Have faith in yourself and your abilities to respond to new information.
✓ Don't take it personally when the future is not what you expected.
✓ Have trust in your intuition.
✓ Prepare for multiple outcomes.
✓ Look for opportunities in change.
✓ Watch for early signals of change.
✓ When worry sets in, focus on your successes.

EXERCISES TO REDUCE WORRY

1. Recognize your worries. Give them a name. Write them down. Describe what physical, mental and emotional signals you get from each worry. This allows you to distance yourself from them. You own them; they no longer own you.
2. Keep a log of your worries. When do you feel worried? Under what conditions? How severe are the worries? Is there a pattern in time, place, condition, or stimulus? What are the themes?
3. What information or help do you need to add perspective to your worries? Prioritize the worries. Which are productive and which are unproductive? Which of the unproductive worries are holding you back the most? When do you experience the generalized "tummy ache" worries about an uncertain future?
4. For productive worries, take action, even if it is a small step towards a final resolution.
5. For unproductive worries, break it down into small, manageable, not so scary pieces. Think about what is the worst that can happen. Probably, it's not that bad. Convert each piece into a productive worry, take action.
6. Try yoga or meditation to relax and relieve the generalized discomfort with uncertainty.

7. Laugh. Find the humor in the situation. Think about how you will retell the story over a glass of wine.
8. Cherish your family, friends, and support system.
9. Think about how you can change your ability to identify details to worry about into a positive to give yourself a specific advantage.
10. Select a particularly upbeat song to be your "theme song" when you are feeling general worry.
11. Have something beautiful in your office, so you can look at it and remind yourself to see the bigger picture. I had a poster of a Renoir painting of two young girls reading together. It reminded me of peace, beauty, and, most important, of the strong bond with my sister. It reminded me that even if the future is unknown, I was not alone.
12. Acknowledge that the future is unknown and uncertain. Think of life as an adventure.

Conclusion

When Roomba's® wheels get gummed up, progress stops. Unproductive worry and discomfort with an uncertain future gums up your progress. Addressing worry takes effort and practice, but the benefit is long term and dramatic.

Chapter 6

When you get stuck, ask for help

In my family room, I have a glider chair that has a round tubular base. Cleaning around this chair is one of Roomba's® biggest challenges. If it approaches head on, its wheels can go over the one inch high circular base, and it gets stuck. Within seconds, with a flashing light and three loud beeps, Roomba® asks for help. I usually run to it, gently lift it off the chair base and set it in an open space. It zooms off in a new direction with renewed energy. As the Roomba® "assistant," I feel that I have helped it reach its goal. I feel strong, needed, and surprisingly connected to Roomba®.

My husband will not ask for directions when we travel. Not even from the voice in the GPS system, affectionately named Jill. Not unusual or unique. It's hard to ask for help. There are three key elements to asking for help: recognizing that you cannot succeed alone; having the fortitude to admit that to someone else in order to ask for help; and having the humility to accept and follow the recommendations of the helper.

We all hesitate to ask for help, for small things as well as for important things. Why?

1. *I don't want to bother anyone.* I can still hear my mother saying "…and what do you want NOW?" We hesitate to ask for help because it may intrude on the other person's time and space. A sincere request for help is different than dumping an unwanted task. The recipient of the request should be honored to be seen as an expert and willing to share that expertise.

2. *I don't want to look weak or dumb.* Asking for help makes us feel inadequate or incapable. This is a particular hurdle for women in business. In fact, asking for help is essential to growth and continued learning. It shows strength, confidence, and courage.

3. *I can solve this on my own.* Confident? Over-confident? Maybe. It could be denial, the "If I ignore the problem, it will go away and I won't have to get help," strategy. Sometimes that works, but we miss the opportunity to solve the problem and learn for the future.

4. *It's not really a problem.* We tend to deny the need for help, sometimes until the problem is so big it just can't be ignored anymore. A good boss, friend or mentor will provide help when you ask, but most do not like cleaning up a mess after it becomes a big problem.

5. *If I ask for help from someone, what if that person says no?* Fear of rejection frequently holds us back from asking for help. Asking for help is a sign of a trusting relationship. Find people you can trust, and develop those reciprocal relationships.

6. *But what if I do ask for help and the person gives the wrong help, sends me in the wrong direction?* Trusting others in time of need is very difficult, but is essential to learning and moving forward. If help is offered, you don't have to take it. You need to use your judgment of the situation and the help to decide.

7. *I don't want to ask for help now because what if things get worse and I need help again? Then I will have used up my resource.* Not really. Trusting mutual relationships are not a zero sum game, where one person gains only if the other loses.

8. *I don't know anyone who can help.* We can underestimate our resources and prevent ourselves from moving forward. If you really don't know someone who can help, work on expanding your network of resources.

9. *What if I ask for help and that person outshines me and makes me look useless?* Recently, I was at a board of directors meeting for a non-profit organization. The Program Director admitted that he was not sure how to proceed on an important project. Another board member offered to write an outline in order to get the project started. The document was so complete, creative, and unusual that the Program Director was outshined. At the next meeting, the other Board members braced for conflict, but the Program Director praised the work and was sincerely grateful. He gained the respect of the entire board because he had the vision of the agency in mind, not his own agenda.

10. *Being self-sufficient is a virtue.* Yes, but so is self-preservation. Is it better to fail alone or succeed with others? Not a tough decision.

When we take apart these "reasons," we see that they are fragile and easily destroyed. That is because they are not really "reasons," but "excuses." In reality, to ask for help is to be strong, visionary, and purposeful.

Hopefully, you are convinced that asking for help is important. How you ask for that help is critical, particularly for women. Shaunti Feldman, in her book, *The Male Factor*, (Feldman, 2009) describes a gender bias in asking for help. Her research indicates that, in general, men tend to do the best they can and depend on their experience and resourcefulness. So, frequently, men will view a request for help from a woman as a sign of weakness and a lack of determination. Women can overcome this unintended reaction if the request for help is appropriate, clear, and timely.

✓ Appropriate. It is appropriate to ask for help in order to achieve an overall organizational goal, not to dump a task that is undesirable. When asking for help, make it clear that you understand the importance of the task and are committed to completing it.

- o Don't: "I'm swamped and Company XX is complaining again. Would you draft the response to this letter for me?"
- o Do: "Company XX is our biggest client so I want our response to be perfect, would you review it for me?"

✓ Clear. Requests must be defined with boundaries and outcomes.

- o Don't: "Glad I ran into you. Take over facilitating the afternoon meeting, okay?"
- o Do: "Tom, thanks for setting aside a few minutes to talk. I have a scheduling conflict because of an emergency meeting with a client. Would you be willing to facilitate the afternoon meeting? I can give you a briefing on the agenda and expected issues."

✓ Timely. If you are asking for help, be sure that you give the person sufficient time to provide the help and sufficient time for you to implement the help and still meet your deadline.

- o Don't: "Sorry for the short notice, but, I need some data on inventory levels in your region for a report that I have to give my boss before lunch today."
- o Do: "I just read over the specifications for this bid request and I will need some information from you in order to submit the bid. It's due in two weeks, so can I get the information within one week?"

✓ Committed. If you ask for help before you try, then it will appear that you didn't put in any effort to solve the problem on your own. Ask for help when you need it, not to make your life easier.

- o Don't: "The boss just handed me this project and I don't know where to start. Can I pick your brain for a while?"
- o Do: "The boss gave me the Smith project. I looked at several approaches but I would value your input before I go in one direction. Can I review my

ideas with you and see if you have more suggestions?"

✓ Make a request, not a demand. If you are making a "request" but you cannot or will not take "no" for an answer, then it is not a request, it is a demand. The response to a true request can be "yes," "no," or "maybe, with a counteroffer," and you have to be willing to accept any of those with graciousness. If you express your request as a demand then be sure you have the authority to make a demand.

o Don't: "No? What do you mean no?"

o Do: "No, I completely understand your time constraints. Can you recommend anyone in the organization who could help on this project?"

EXERCISE IN ASKING FOR HELP

Asking for help in your personal development is a particularly important request. Handling this effectively can demonstrate your commitment to your performance and the organizational goals.

Set aside a few hours twice a year to do a situation analysis.

1. How are you feeling? Happy? Confident? Scared? Bored? Challenged? Underwater? Stressed? Enthusiastic? Overworked?

2. List the skills you have used effectively in the past six months. Which of these can you develop further? How will you accomplish that? What help do you need to enhance these skills? Who can help you?

3. List the skills you needed but did not have in the past six months. How can you gain these skills? What skill development is the highest priority? What actions should you take now? What help do you need to gain these skills? Who should you ask?

4. Look forward to the next six months. What new

skills will you need to be successful? How can you access these skills? What help do you need? Who can provide the help?

5. What skills would you like to have to accelerate your personal and professional growth? How will you get them? Who can help you?

6. What is the next step that you want for your career? What new skills will you need? Which of your current skills will become more important and need to be upgraded? How will you accomplish this? Who can help you?

7. Sit down with your supervisor at work and ask what he or she would see as your next career step and what you need to accomplish it. Do an action plan.

8. Six months later, review your plans and see what you accomplished (congratulations!) and what you still need to do. Think about what made you successful in some items and not so successful in others. What help do you need to improve your stats?

9. View all advice and help with an open, mindful, and non-critical head and heart.

Conclusion

When Roomba® gets stuck, it recognizes that this problem is more than it can overcome alone. It asks for help and accepts the help. It could not succeed in accomplishing its overall goals without doing so. Keep your overall vision and goal in mind and ask for help. You do not have to do it all alone. Being a help "asker" or a help "giver" creates a special bond. Value that bond as much as you value the help.

Chapter 7

When you have a tough problem, keep on top of it

Roomba® has an interesting feature. If it detects some dirt that's more challenging than normal, a little blue light flashes and it spins in a tight circle over the dirt until it is clean. It doesn't continue on its mission until the spot is clean. When faced with a tough problem, Roomba® keeps on top of it.

Most of us are not like Roomba®. We tend to avoid the really difficult tasks, procrastinate, and hope they will go away. We do that because we are afraid that we will fail, that we are not sure exactly what to do, we overestimate the difficulty of the project, we want to wait until we can do it perfectly, and sometimes because we just can't face that big hairy monster of a task. So, instead, we busy ourselves with other, less scary, less daunting, but way less important things.

Tim, a young executive, felt challenged with too much to accomplish in too little time. He told me that he felt like he was running in place and always on the edge of failure. Not an unusual problem, and certainly not a fun way to work. He felt that he needed a better system for time management, so he dove into an elaborate "to do" system. When I met him, he showed me page after page of tasks, many crossed off, many repeated day after day, and still he was missing deadlines and always putting out fires. His lists were so comprehensive that I almost expected to see "lunch" on the list. When I asked how he decided which tasks to do first, he said that some days he started at the top but most days he did the easiest things first so he could cross them off the list and feel good when he counted up the number of check marks at the end of the day. He forgot that his success did not depend on getting something done; it depended on getting the *right* things done.

The Pareto Principle, which was developed by the Italian economist, Vilfredo Pareto, is also known as the 80 – 20 rule. He showed that 80% of desired results flow from 20% of our activities. That means that 80% of Tim's effectiveness depends on selecting the important 20% of the things on his "to do" list, and then doing them right.

Steven R. Covey, in his book, *The 7 Habits of Highly Effective People*, (Covey, 1989) describes in *Habit 3, Put First Things First*, a simple, but very effective way of making sure the right things get done. He uses a quadrant system, and categorizes tasks using two parameters; urgency and importance. In the first quadrant are things that are urgent and important. These are the items with the earliest deadlines that are critical to success, certainly part of the 20%. These are the things to conquer first. In the second quadrant are items that are not urgent but are important. These things fall into the 20%, but you have some time to do them. They should be your second priority so they get done before they move into the first, urgent, quadrant. The third quadrant has things that are urgent but not important. They are the time stealers like phone calls, emails, and interruptions. These items need to be actively managed so they don't take up all your time but are done effectively. And, finally in the fourth quadrant are things that are not urgent and not important. These are things we shouldn't be doing at all. Just say no to them.

Randy Pausch, best known for his video and book *The Last Lecture*, did a lecture at University of Virginia on time management. Both videos are available on his website (Randy Pausch's website, 2007). He points out that time is a commodity, much like money, except that you can get more money but you can't get more time. People typically waste about two hours in their work day because they can't find things, are unprepared, distracted, or bored. If you spend time on things that don't really matter, there is an opportunity cost. You don't have that time to spend on the things that do matter. He elaborates on Steven Covey's system by telling us to ask the questions, "Why am I doing this?" and "What will happen if I don't do it at all?" Then, he reminds us to "get the monkey off your back" and do the ugliest task first. If you have two ugly tasks on your list, do the ugliest one first.

Another approach to prioritizing is described by Brian Tracy in *Eat That Frog* (Tracy, 2001). He has three easy (?) steps to ending procrastination and getting the right things done:

1. If the first thing you do each morning is to eat a live frog, you can go through the day with the satisfaction of knowing that this is probably the worst thing that is going to happen to you all day long.
2. If you have to eat two frogs, eat the ugliest first.
3. If you have to eat a live frog, it does not pay to sit and look at it for very long.

His message is to get the hardest, most important things done first, and the rest of the day looks great in comparison.

These and many other sources can give you valuable tools so you can take on the tough problems and prioritize your work. So, what's holding you back?

Unfortunately, many of us are not sure how we spend our time. I have often heard colleagues say "I don't know where the day went," or "It's five o'clock and I feel like the past four hours slipped away." So, the first step is to find out how you are spending your time. A recent article in the *Wall Street Journal* titled *Employees, Measure Yourselves* (Wilson, 2012), describes many tools for self-monitoring, from tracking screen times, measuring time spent on websites, hourly reminders to keep you on track, to web-based "to do" systems. But the good old pen and paper will work as well. Monitor your hour-by-hour activities and accomplishments to see how you are spending your time.

The next big decision is how you will prioritize your tasks. Using importance and urgency is a good place to start, but you need to define these terms for your own situation.

Write down a clear definition of important and urgent in your work, taking into consideration the following elements:

Important

✓ Important to whom? To the company? To your boss? To you?
✓ What makes it important? Impact on the bottom line? Impact on customers? Impact on compliance with regulations?
✓ What happens if it doesn't get done? How big is the impact?
✓ What is the benefit if it does get done?
✓ How good is good enough?

Urgent

✓ How urgent is this task? Today? This week? This month?
✓ Is it feasible to get it done in the required time or do I need to notify someone?
✓ How solid is the deadline? Is it a real deadline or an artificial one?
✓ How fast will the deadline move?
✓ What is the impact of missing the deadline? Is it an all-or-nothing deadline?
✓ What will be the impact if the task is done ahead of schedule?

Another method of prioritizing (Tracy, 2001) is the ABCDE method.

✓ **A** is a task that is very important and that you must do. There is a significant negative impact if you put this off.
✓ **B** is a task that is important, but not as important as an "A" task. There may be some consequences if it is not done.
✓ **C** is a task that is nice to do, but not as important as either "A" or "B" tasks, and there are no negative consequences if it is not done.
✓ **D** is a task that you should delegate or outsource.
✓ **E** is a task that should not be done.

Some of my clients used different colors of sticky notes on tasks to remind them of priorities. One of my clients had a table in her office that she divided into the four quadrants with tape and put tasks, memos and reports into the proper quadrant. She reviewed quadrant 2 (important but not urgent) pile each day to see if something should be moved to quadrant 1 (important and urgent). Using physical cues as a reminder of priorities is a valuable tool.

These methods will help you prioritize your activities by what is important and what should be done first. Now you need to match those priorities with your own focus and energy rhythms. If you are a morning person, go ahead and eat that big hairy purple frog at 8:00 am. But if morning is not when your energy is at its peak, postpone the frog snack until you are best suited to eat it successfully. I am not a morning person. (My husband is laughing.) I am at my best and most productive just after lunch. My daily routine is to start off with those tasks that are urgent but not important, the "C" tasks, the emails, letters, and phone calls. Then I start the tasks that are important but not urgent, the "B" tasks. That gives me time to look at them again before the deadline. In the early afternoon, I am ready to eat the frog, the "A" tasks. I can focus and be most productive until about 6:00 pm. Balance your "to do" list against your "can do" schedule to be the most productive.

In a perfect workplace, we would be able to set up our schedule and accomplish all the tasks without interruptions or new priorities. Not so in the real world. In my business of analytical testing, priorities changed hour by hour. It was like an emergency room for testing of water, wastewater, and food samples. Clients needed rush analyses to make decisions and we responded as best and as quickly as we could. In some cases, public health and safety were at stake. It was my responsibility to approach my already stretched scientists and ask them to change their schedules to handle a rush order. I told them that they had three choices when I asked them for "a small favor for a client." They could say "yes, no problem," or "no, it can't get done because of an unchangeable factor," or "yes, but then I have to change another priority, and would that be acceptable?" It was the third answer that happened most frequently and was most valuable. It opened the door to clear and complete communication of expectations. When changes occur, look for the ripple effect on all other priorities. Clearly communicate the impact to others who would be affected by the change.

EXERCISE IN SETTING PRIORITIES

1. Find out how you are spending your time. What are your time wasters, and how can they be minimized? What tasks are you doing efficiently, and where else can you use that technique? Where are you least efficient, and how can you minimize it?
2. Define the criteria you will use to prioritize tasks.
3. Be sure to get rid of the tasks that are not necessary – just say "no."
4. Define your peak personal energy blocks.
5. Set up your task calendar with day, week, month, quarter, and year segments.
6. Use the task calendar to monitor progress.

Conclusion

Roomba® works smart, not hard. It takes on the tough problems and still succeeds in getting the whole job done. Prioritize and attack your tough tasks. Work smarter, not harder!

Chapter 8

Success is not a straight line

One day I decided to challenge Roomba®. I put it into a small bedroom and scattered ten pieces of colored paper, each about a quarter of an inch square, around the room. I pressed "clean" and waited. It took a while, but Roomba® succeeded in picking up all ten pieces. During the process, it crossed the room over thirty times, changing direction, spinning around chair legs, doing its circle dance in the middle of the room and hugging the baseboards. Not a straight line, but very successful.

If you check the definition of "success" in the dictionary, it will be described as a favorable or desired outcome, or more commonly, the attainment of wealth. That's one way to look at it. But from the big picture, the whole life view, it is much more profound than just the attainment of wealth. It encompasses all of your hopes and dreams for yourself and for those you love. That vision evolves as you journey through your life and career. Success is the achievement of happiness.

Success is not an event that happens by linear progression. Instead, it unfolds on many different levels simultaneously. This happens partially because we define success in many domains, using both internal and external metrics. In addition, we change our definition of success as we get closer to it. And, we change our definition of success as we change our definition of ourselves.

Success is very personal. It is what makes you happy. Your definition is very different from mine. Defining success in all the relevant domains, and then challenging yourself to reach for success will distinguish you from the crowd. Anna Quindlen, a Pulitzer Prize winning author, journalist, and opinion columnist, describes her meandering, non-linear path to success and happiness in her recent memoir (Quindlen, 2012). She describes the years she spent raising her siblings after her mother died, her initial firm stance to never have children of her own, her focus on her career as a journalist, her about-face on motherhood, followed by the birth of her three children and finding her true self in family and writing. She has observed that frequently people define success by what some amorphous "they, out there" define as success rather than having the courage to follow their own dreams.

Last semester I was teaching an undergraduate course in the Entrepreneurship department of a major university. One of the assignments I gave the students was to write the essence of their personal definition of success by writing what they want on their tombstone. Catlyn said that she had grown up very poor and so she wanted her tombstone to read, "Made lots of money, shared it wisely." Tom, a football player from a broken home wanted his to read, "A good man." He told the class of his definitions of "good" and "man," and how those two words summarized everything that was important to him. A highly driven young woman, Beth, wanted the words, "Started, built, and ran the most powerful company in the country." A young man who was working his way through school while supporting an extended family wanted, "Family, God, Country, in that order," so his legacy reflected his strong commitments. A woman with a great sense of humor said, "Loving daughter, wife, mother, and also ran a super business; we're not sure how she did it all, while laughing all the way." A dedicated student from the education department said, "A teacher who impacted many." And, the shortest, but possibly the most impactful, was from a man who summarized his definition of life and success as, "he was happy." These examples capture the depth and breadth of the definition of success for these young people today. I challenged them to keep this epitaph in a safe place and re-read it in ten years.

A recent movie, *New Year's Eve* (Marshall, 2011), showed another perspective on the definition of success. In the beginning of the movie, the character played by Michele Pfeiffer, is busily hunched over her desk in the late afternoon of New Year's Eve. A messenger who is delivering an envelope with the invitations to the most prestigious event of the evening, jokes with her that she is putting a lot of effort into her New Year's resolutions. After a quick denial, she admits, that yes, this is her resolution list. Next scene, a depressing interaction with her boss is followed by her resignation. She challenges the messenger that if he can give her everything on her list before midnight he can have the lusted-after tickets. He takes the challenge. He takes every one of her seemingly impossible wishes and makes it happen. By the end she understands that it is important to define success for herself, but also to be open to new ways to reach that success and to embrace it when it happens. For the cute details, check out the film.

Last year, I was asked to teach a seminar course at a university with the challenging topic of Gender Issues in Entrepreneurship. There are reams of data from international sources concluding that, all things being equal, a woman is less likely than a man to start an entrepreneurial venture. The statistics show that:

✓ Although women own 30% of privately-owned businesses in the United States, this accounts for only 11% of sales and 13% of employment.
✓ Average sales for a business owned by a woman are 25% of the sales in businesses owned by a man. Women-owned businesses are much smaller than male-owned businesses, on average.
✓ Women start with less capital and take on less debt than men do.
✓ The annual earnings ratio between entrepreneurial women and men is 55%. This means that for every dollar earned by a male entrepreneur, a female entrepreneur earns only fifty-five cents.
✓ Educational backgrounds for men and women entrepreneurs are similar.
✓ Women generally preferred low risk/low return businesses.
✓ Women entrepreneurs tend to be older than men entrepreneurs when they start their businesses.

Throughout the sixteen weeks of the class, the eleven women and four men in the class dug into possible explanations using a wide variety of research sources and interviews of successful women entrepreneurs. They investigated structural barriers, educational inequities, financial challenges, network and mentoring limitations, differences in managerial style or teambuilding, family responsibilities, and definitions of success. Most of the students admitted that they hoped to find a definitive reason for the difference. They wanted to uncover societal barriers that are challenging obstacles for women. They wanted to be able to throw up their hands and yell, "See, women have been repressed!" The real conclusions were interesting, encouraging, and very surprising. The conclusions were:

- ✓ In the past there were structural barriers for women, such as more difficult access to capital, harder to find an entrepreneurial mentor, less family support, and less access to technical education. However, these barriers have been disappearing at a rapid rate, but the rate of women entrepreneurs and the types of businesses started by these women have not changed.
- ✓ The key difference is that men and women have different definitions of success.
  Women defined success through a balance of achievement, recognition, and personal relationships. They focused on mastery of the subject matter, building strong organizations, doing enjoyable work, and finding personal fulfillment. Men defined success through material success, mostly financial success. They focused on power, business growth, status in the community, and money as a measure of success. (Dyke & Murphy, 2006) The surprising fact is that women's entrepreneurship appears to lag only when compared to the yardstick of male-based entrepreneurship. The encouraging conclusion is that women start and run successful businesses that fit their own definitions of success.

The 12 Domains of Success

Watch TV, read a best-selling novel, hang out at the gym, and you will get the popular definition of success, a new car, a bigger house, great biceps, an honor roll son or daughter, or a promotion to vice president. But real success is not just one thing, it's a lot of things simultaneously that are balanced precariously. Many of the following domains of success can overlap, can be complementary or can be in conflict. The twelve domains of success fall into three categories: self-focused domains, relationship-focused domains, and world-focused domains.

Self-focused Domains

1. Achievement – The most commonly thought of domain of success is achievement, what you have accomplished in the past and what you strive to accomplish in the future. Achievement can be reflected in your career path, degrees you have earned, professional accolades, or notoriety in your field. This is the easiest domain to measure with concrete metrics and the ability to set goals that are definable.
   a. Example: Last year I finished my MBA and have achieved the level of product manager in my organization. I want to reach the level of business area manager within five years.
2. Enhancement of a personal quality or attribute – This may be a vocation, avocation, or personal trait that you want to enhance and develop.
   a. Example: I would be successful in this domain if I fully develop my capabilities as a mentor for new members of the staff by completing a mentorship and coaching training program and effectively use the techniques to impact others.
3. What you have – The stuff, including the type of house, the car, clothes, and accessories.

      a. Example: I will feel successful in this domain if I have a house that will be safe and comfortable for my spouse and two children.

4. What you want to experience – This domain encompasses the experiences that you want to have, such as traveling, living in a different culture, participating in a competitive sport, moving to a new city, hearing music, or getting married.

      a. Example: Each year I want to vacation in a new place, and open myself to the experiences of that place, the culture, and the people.

5. Physical – How you care for yourself physically. In this domain you have an image of your best physical self, and you decide how you will achieve and maintain that.

      a. Example: I will eat a healthy diet to maintain my weight, even when I am traveling on business or during tax season, but maybe let myself indulge a bit during my vacation.

6. What you want to stop doing – Success sometimes means not doing something that prevents you from succeeding in another domain. Quitting smoking helps a commitment to live a healthy lifestyle.

      a. Example: I will stop eating lunch at my desk. I will benefit from a break from work. I'll eat better foods and enjoy them more.

Relationship-focused Domains

7. What you mean to others – This domain describes what you want in your close personal relationships, including your parents, your spouse, children, colleagues, and close friends.

      a. Example: I want my parents to know that they can count on me to help them to comfortably stay in their home for as long as possible.

8. How are you seen by others – Some individuals seek the limelight, while others prefer the background. But both are concerned about how they are seen by others.

This domain of success is what you see when your profile is reflected to you by others.

  a. Example: I want others to see me as generous, caring, and trusting, but certainly not a pushover.

World-focused Domains

9. Who you are in terms of your purpose and where you find meaning in your life – This definition of success reflects your deeper commitment to become a purposeful participant in society.

  a. Example: I will feel successful in this domain if I live each day with integrity.

10. What you give away – Philanthropy and volunteerism. Sharing time, money and expertise is a critical definition of success for many people.

  a. Example: I want to be able to donate one week a year to Engineers without Borders in order to bring my expertise to others.

11. How you impact the world – For some individuals, the ability to put their stamp on the greater community is very important. For others, it is sufficient to be part of a close-knit neighborhood.

  a. Example: I want to serve as a County Commissioner, with the hope of preserving open space in my community.

12. Spirituality – This domain describes your definition of success in relation to your religious or spiritual beliefs.

  a. Example: I will live as a good Christian.

How do you define success?

Your personal definition of success will be based on some, most, or all of the above domains. The emphasis will change as you reach your goals in some areas and as your life changes. It's okay, no, *critical*, to change and evolve your vision of success as you move through life.

✓ Mary, a young executive I recently coached, had spent the last eight years working at an extreme pace, with extensive travel, while completing an executive MBA program. As you can guess, her definition of success included achievement, increasing what she had, and enhancing her personal abilities. Now, one year into a marriage and anticipating her first child, she is balancing her success goals with that of her husband and looking towards spending more time with her family (enhancing personal relationships and stopping the extensive business travel). At first she struggled with the thought that she was "copping out" of the "career track" to go to a "mommy track." However, she realized that she had the right, even the obligation, to change her definition of success as her life and relationships changed.

Mary's First Success Wheel

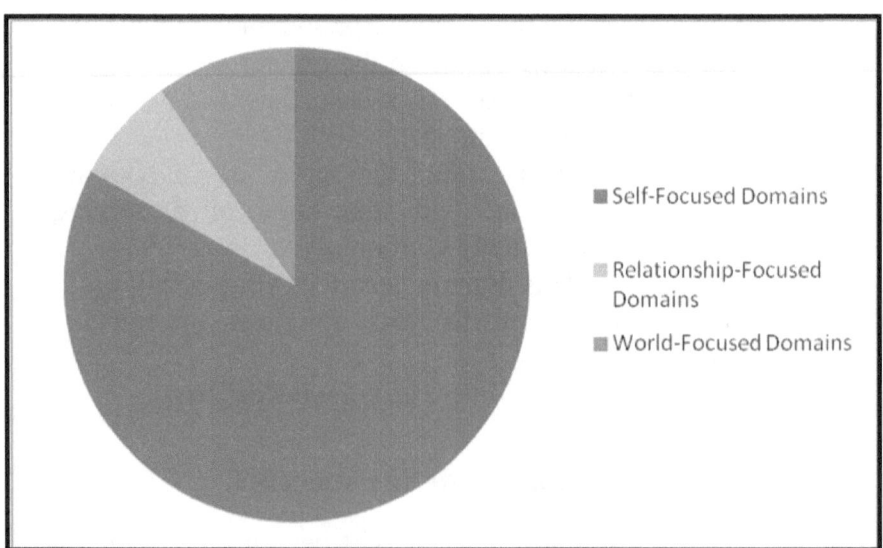

Mary's new success wheel

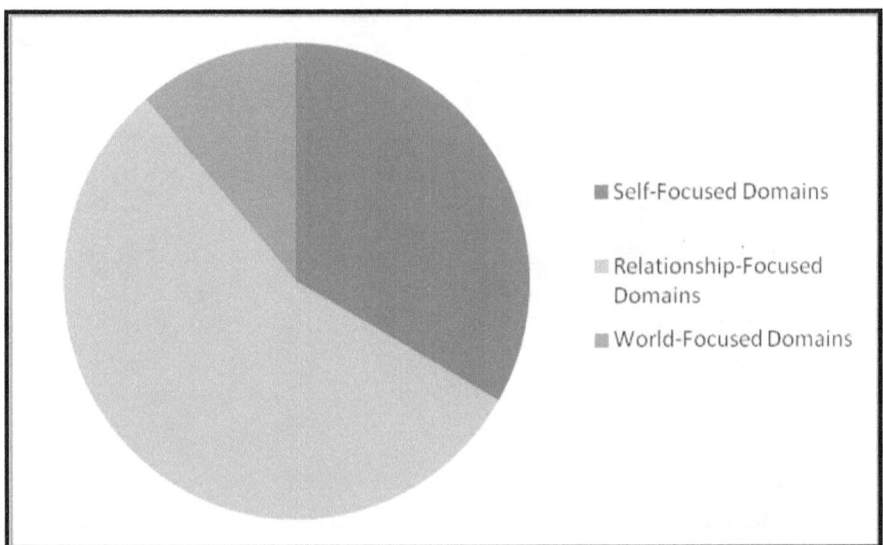

- ✓ Edward had built an amazing career in health care administration, culminating in a five year contract as the CEO of a major health network. As age 65 approached and he contemplated retirement, he knew he had to change his definition of success. In what he called "act 2," he focused on streamlining the operations of a non-profit organization and mentoring young executives. His new definition of success had "create purpose and meaning," "relationships with others," and "what you give away," as key components.

Edward's original success wheel

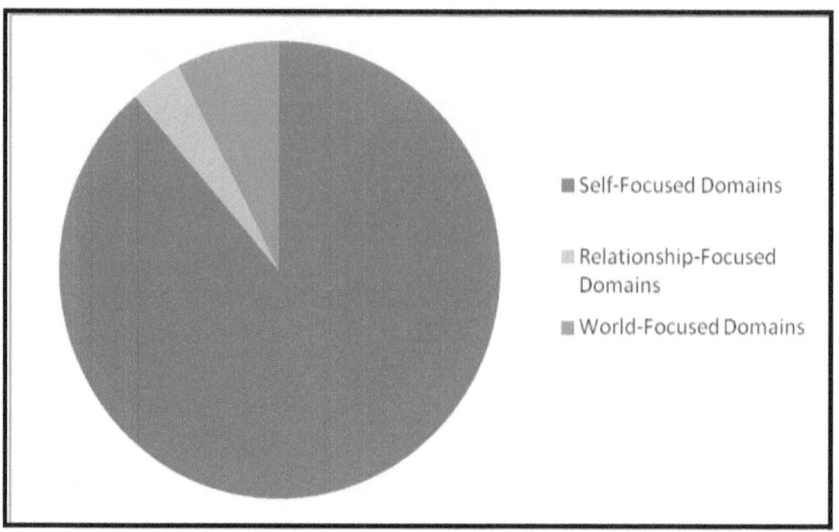

Edward's new success wheel

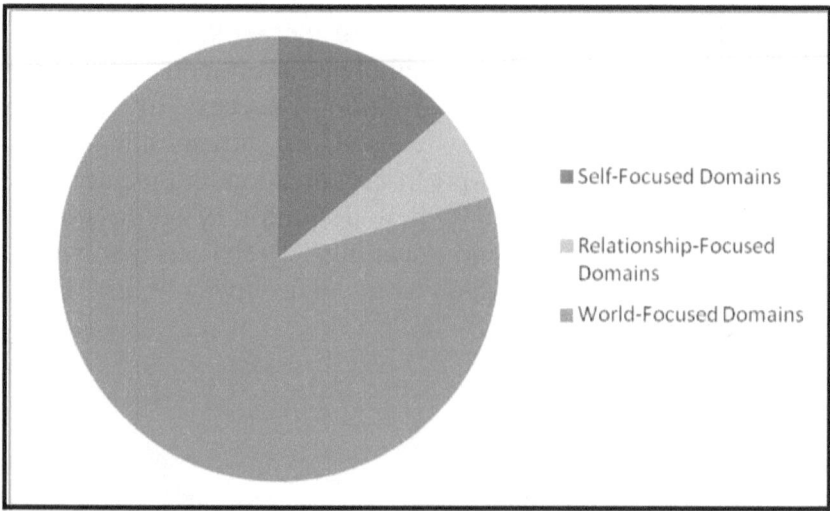

✓ Jonathan grew up in a tough section of a major city. In high school, his definition of success was just to stay alive. After winning an athletic scholarship to college and landing a high-potential job, he went back to his neighborhood to establish a basketball league in the basement of his church. His focus shifted to "achievement," "personal enhancement," and "how he would be seen by the neighborhood."

Jonathan's original success wheel

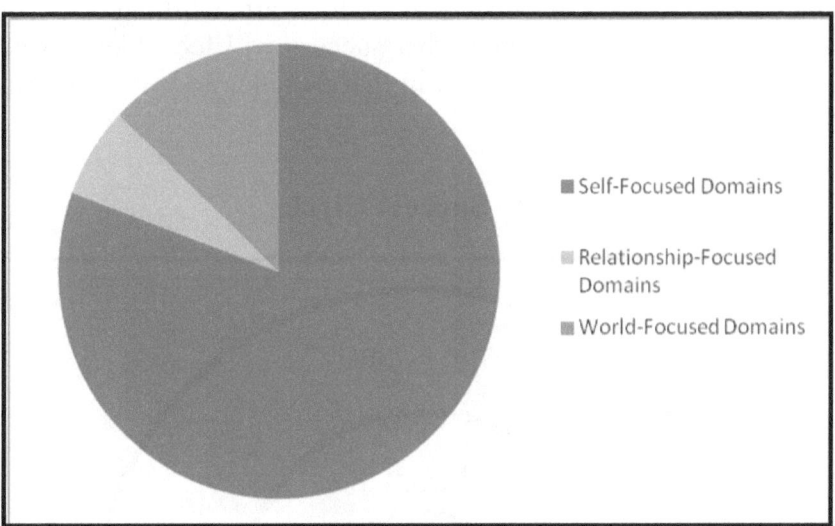

Jonathan's new success wheel

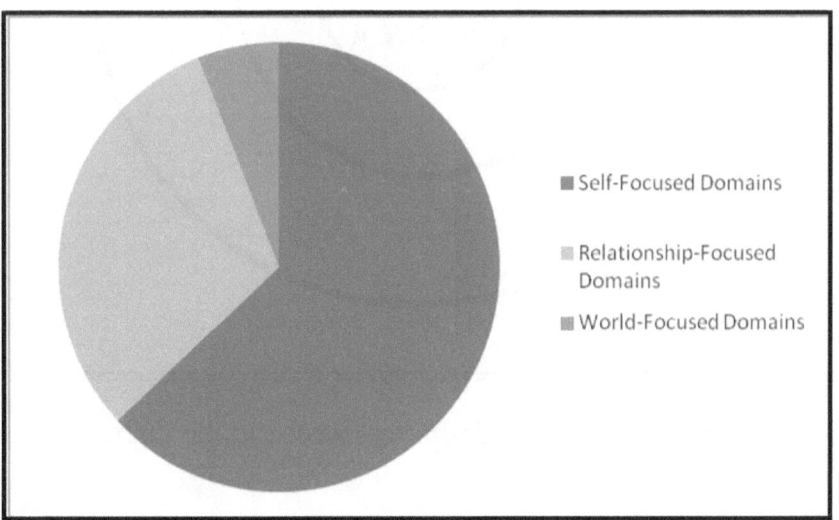

Describing Success

In each of the twelve domains described above there are three dimensions. That is, what you want success to look like, why you want to achieve this goal, and what it will feel like when you achieve it. A natural tendency is to start working on your definitions by thinking about what success will look like. Wrong. Start with how you want to feel in that domain, and work outward from there.

The Success Circle

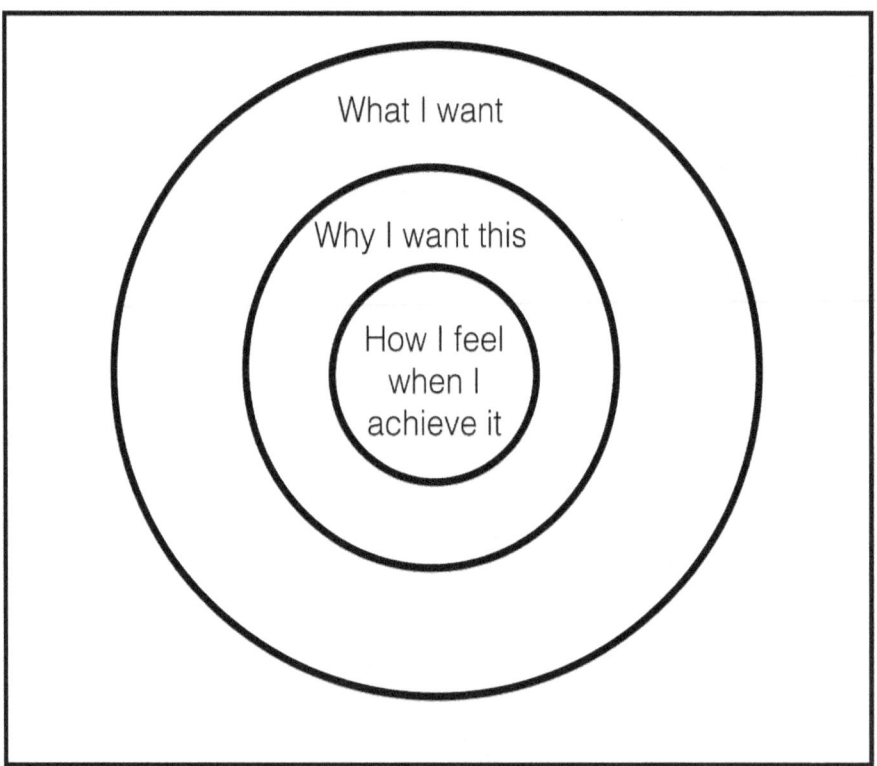

If we go back to Edward's desire to succeed in the domain, "what you give away:"

✓ He wanted to *feel* the joy of sharing.
✓ He *wanted to do it* in order to impact the new organization, the customers of the non-profit, and the next generation of young executives.
✓ He realized that the culmination of his professional career was that he had accumulated knowledge, wisdom, and resources that he could apply in a new direction.

Jonathan's desire to be seen by others as setting an example:

✓ He wanted to *feel* that he was deeply connected to his family, friends, and neighborhood in a positive way.
✓ He *wanted to do it* in order to be a role model for others and to see other kids succeed.
✓ He wanted to mentor and teach at-risk kids from his neighborhood, using the resources he was able to accumulate.

By building each domain of success in this way, a deep understanding and commitment to success eases the way when things get tough. If you understand what domains of success were important to you in the past, you will have a better understanding of how you got to where you are now. Projecting into the future, and asking yourself what domains of success will become more important to you in the next five and ten years will help you plan for your long-term happiness.

Recognize that success is not a straight line. It changes and evolves. Your success wheel will continue to evolve as you redefine yourself and your future.

EXERCISE IN DEFINING SUCCESS

Create your own success wheel.
1. Select the first domain of success, and ask yourself how you would want to feel if you were successful in this domain. Describe why you want to feel this way. Outline what you would have to do to make this happen.

2. Continue through all the domains. Be honest, and take the time to really think about each one.
3. On a spreadsheet program, list the twelve domains of success. Based on the above, give each category a score of 1 to 10 with 1 being least important to you and 10 being most important to you. You can have many domains with the same number. They do not have to add up to a specific total.
4. Use the graph function for a pie chart, and visualize your success wheel. Group the domains into the three categories then look at them individually for a more detailed picture.
5. Think back over the past five years. How would your success wheel be different five years ago? How about ten years ago? What factors or influences changed your definition of success?
6. Think ahead for a five and ten-year period. How will your success wheel change over that time period? Why? What can you do now to achieve success in the domains that will become more important to your happiness in the future?
7. Review and update your success wheel at least once a year, maybe with your New Year's Resolutions.

Conclusion

Roomba's® definition of success focuses on "achievement" and "relationship with others," obvious from its focus on thoroughly cleaning the entire space, not disturbing my cats unnecessarily, and giving me precious free time so I can focus on my own definitions of success. Is Roomba® successful and happy? I can almost see a smile on its face!

Chapter 9

Do the right thing, especially when nobody is watching

One of the real benefits of having Roomba® is that I can set it in motion in a room and leave, so I am free to do other things. Whether I am "supervising" it or not, Roomba® works with the same diligence and effectiveness. It doesn't slack off, cut corners, or take an extended coffee break. It does the right thing, even when I'm not watching.

Integrity is doing the right thing even when nobody is watching, even if you would never get caught. Living a life of integrity is the greatest goal you can have. Integrity is essential to establishing trust, and is vital to the reputation of the individual and the organization. It encompasses the moral values of honesty, truthfulness, and fairness. Unfortunately, in recent years there have been so many examples of a lack of integrity in business and politics that we are becoming desensitized to the impact. In our nation, serious integrity, ethical, and moral issues are in the newspaper every day, including corporate scandals, accounting fraud, steroid use in baseball, immorality in religious organizations, crimes by trusted mentors, and political careers ended in scandal. But just because someone famous did it, or it happens all the time, is neither an excuse, nor a justification for it to continue. Change starts with one person, and that should be you.

Ethics and business ethics are taught in colleges and universities across the country. In addition, there has been a major push in corporations to write and publicize their organizational ethical code. These efforts focus on the major ethical values; honesty, promise-keeping, loyalty, fairness, concern for others, respect for others, law abiding, pursuit of excellence, and personal accountability. They describe the principled reasoning steps to ethical decision-making; clarify, evaluate, decide, implement, monitor, and modify.

So, if ethical conduct is so easy to describe and so well communicated, why do we still fail to reach the goal of behaving with integrity? In some cases, individuals rationalize their decisions.

- ✓ Well, it's not illegal. I'm just fighting fire with fire.
- ✓ He did it first.
- ✓ I only did it once.
- ✓ Nobody got hurt so what's the big deal?
- ✓ If everybody is doing it, it can't be wrong.
- ✓ I deserved it.
- ✓ They didn't need it.

These rationalizations are attempts to justify an action or behavior that the individual "knew" was wrong, usually for personal gain.

In 2008, Ron Alsop (Alsop, 2008) published his studies of how the millennial generation, those born between 1980 and 2001, are changing the workplace. This is the generation that is now entering the workforce. He described this generation as technology savvy, intolerant of ambiguity, uncomfortable with risk or independent decision-making, civic-minded, high self-esteem, close parental ties, high expectations, and committed to a work/life balance. In his research, he compared values of those in the millennial generation to other generations, and categorized them into six values groups: theoretical (discovery of truth), economic (accumulation of goods and wealth), aesthetic (idealism and beauty), social (humanistic, unselfish), political (power, influence, and status), and religious (spirituality and peace). For those in the millennial generation, economic values ranked the highest with both males and females, while religious values scored the lowest. His conclusions are that the millennial generation places more value on the accumulation of wealth than on any other value area, and that our business culture is trending towards values that are more individualistic and less societal. He expresses the concern that our culture is trending away from integrity and towards personal gain. However, the work of Erhard, Jensen, and Zaffron (Erhard, Jensen, & Zaffron, 2009), shows how integrity and moral behavior lead to increased performance, better quality of life, and value creation for individuals, groups, organizations, and societies. So there is personal and organizational benefit to moving towards a culture built on integrity.

Integrity is not easy. Doing the right thing, even when nobody is looking, has three key elements. First, *do* the *right* thing. This is different from *not doing* the *wrong* thing. It is being proactive. So, if you see that a co-worker who comes in late almost every day, but fills in her timesheet as if she was on time, ignoring it because it is not you who's doing the cheating, is not enough. Integrity is taking positive action to correct the situation by talking to the co-worker or to her supervisor. Integrity is doing the right thing *no matter who is watching,* not only if "somebody important" is watching. So, whether it is a stranger on the street or your pastor who is watching, it doesn't matter. True integrity is when you do the right thing, even if it is a nameless, faceless, victimless wrong.

The most difficult of the key elements is the word "right." How do you know what is the right thing to do? Integrity, for an individual, a group, or an organization, is defined as:

- ✓ Honoring your word to *yourself* - doing what you say you would do, in the time frame that you said you would do it. This involves self-discipline and self-respect. If you don't honor your word to yourself, you will show up to others as inconsistent, unfocused, scattered, unreliable, undependable, unpredictable, and generally unsatisfied with yourself. When you do honor your word to yourself, you will maintain yourself as a whole and complete person, so you are empowered to deal with others with integrity.
- ✓ Honoring your word to *others* - doing what you say you would do, in the time frame that you said you would do it. If you don't honor your word to others, you will be seen as unreliable, untrustworthy, and dishonest. Your word to others is the basis of a relationship, and an expression of who you are as a

person. Honoring your word to others is the cornerstone of being trustworthy.

✓ As soon as you know that you will not honor your word, you clearly and openly say that you will not honor your word.

✓ You clean up any mess that you caused for those who were counting on your word.

What does "honoring your word" mean? It is not just following through when you give an explicit promise to an individual, it encompasses all of the following:

✓ What you said – whatever you said that you would do or not do. When it is a commitment to do something, then completing it when you said you would do it. If you say that you will have the sales report available for the staff meeting in one week, then you have given your word to have this done, to the best of your ability, and meet the deadline.

✓ What you know you should do – These are the things that you know you should do or not do, without explicitly stating that you will or will not do them. And, in the case of doing something, then it means completing it on time, and doing it the way that it should be done. You know that you should give 100% effort to your employer, and not waste business time on personal emails, internet shopping, or searching for another job. You know you should act with professionalism when you are at a sales conference because, even during happy hour, you represent your organization. And, yes, you know you should take proactive actions when you see a co-worker cheating the organization.

✓ What is expected of you – These are the things that are expected that you will do or not do because of your position, title, level of responsibility, or affiliations. For example, if you have a job that requires an accreditation or certification with a specification for continuing education, then you know that maintaining that accreditation is expected for your continued employment. Although you might not tell your supervisor that you intend to complete the continuing education hours, it is expected that you will do so in a timely manner. If you do not, then you have violated honoring your word because it was reasonably expected that you would do so. If you are a member of a profession with a code of conduct, then you are expected to follow that code without exception.

✓ What you say is so – If you tell others that a certain condition or requirement generally exists, then you should demonstrate that you are in compliance with that requirement yourself. If you expect others to comply with a general requirement, then you should do so yourself to set the example. If you are teaching students that eating healthy foods is important, don't pull out a chocolate bar and 64-ounce, sugary soda for a snack. If you profess that customer service is key to your company's success, don't grumble and gossip about the difficult customer you hope would go elsewhere.

✓ What you say you stand for – Whether you state this to yourself or to others, when you hold yourself out as standing for a principle, then that declaration is part of your word. If you are a member of Mothers Against Drunk Drivers, don't drink and drive, even a little bit, even if you "know" you can handle it. If you are against bullying in any situation, then never sit back and let it happen because you don't want to get involved.

✓ The moral, ethical and legal standards that impact you – Part of your word is that you will abide by the social standards, the ethical standards and the governmental legal requirements of right and wrong behavior in your society, group, or organization. Without this key part, the rest of the definition of integrity can lead to a paradox. For example, the Latin King Gang members honor their word to each other, but they are missing this key requirement of abiding by the legal, moral, and ethical standards of society. Is that integrity?

> Absolutely not. The foundation of integrity is your word that you will live in accordance with the legal, moral, and ethical standards of your community.

Integrity requires that the individual has a unified set of legal, ethical and moral standards that guide decisions and actions when faced with dilemmas. The legal standards are the system of laws and regulations that describe right and wrong behavior in society that are enforceable by the governing body (state, local, federal jurisdictions), using policing and judicial processes with the threat and use of penalties. The legal regulations are readily available through laws and statutes. An integral part of integrity is honoring the legal standards of the community.

Moral standards are generally defined as the principles of right and wrong or good and bad behavior in society. They are less codified than legal standards, but are usually universally understood and accepted. Calling out sick from work in order to play golf is not illegal, but it is generally accepted as not moral. Hiring a marginally qualified new employee only because he or she is related to you, is not illegal, but probably not moral. These are the decisions that we think of as right versus wrong decisions.

Ethical standards are the most difficult to describe because they are judgments in the grey area. Rushworth M. Kidder, in his book, *How Good People Make Tough Choices* (Kidder, 1995), describes four types of ethical dilemmas.

Truth vs. Loyalty

Truth is information that is based on facts or reality, so it is accurate, complete, and relevant. Loyalty is based on allegiance to a person, group, organization, set of ideas, or governing body. It is right to support the truth. It is right to be loyal. So when you face a truth versus loyalty dilemma, you are pushed into a right versus right decision.

✓ Saturday night you had dinner with your sister, Sue, and her husband, Tom. They were excited to announce that they were putting their house on the market and buying a much larger home with a pool. They felt confident that Tom's career was on the verge of taking off and they could afford the much higher mortgage. Tom works in a division of your company in the neighboring town. As Chief Financial Officer of the corporation, you are aware that the company President has been working on divesting that division but the information is highly confidential. It is your understanding that the new owners of the division will probably close the facility and incorporate the operations into their existing facilities in order to get economies of scale. You don't know whether Tom's job will be transferred, but you doubt it. If word about the potential sale got out, it could tank the deal. Do you tell Tom to hold off on buying the new house until the sale becomes public and he knows about his employment status? Or, do you honor your requirement to keep company information confidential? Are you loyal to your sister and her family, or do you keep your word to your boss?

Individual vs. Community

This dilemma can be thought of as the "us versus them," or "self versus others" conflict. Do we decide in favor of the individual, or determine what is best for the group? Individualism assumes that in a society where each person vigorously pursues their own interests, social benefit will automatically happen. Community interests means that the needs of the majority outweigh the interests of the individual. Both of these concepts have merit.

✓ Mary began volunteering at the thrift shop that supported a charitable organization in her community dedicated to helping disabled individuals. All the items in the shop were donated, but were in good condition and very inexpensive. She was told that volunteers are not paid for their work but do get a 50% discount on anything they buy in the shop. On her first day in the shop she was told that one of the charity's board members was a vice president of a large clothing manufacturer, and every other month he had a truck full of donations delivered to the shop. The items were overstocked designer clothes, new and very expensive items that the shop used to lure customers in with the hope of getting bargains. All the volunteers were told the schedule of when the truck would arrive and they got the pick of the items before the rest was put onto the shelves. The volunteer supervisor felt that giving the rest of the volunteers' first choice was their "payment" for the work they did. Mary was not comfortable with buying goods at half price when the items could sell for more to the general public. Should she take advantage of the opportunity to get new, designer clothes at a very low price, or hope they would bring in more money for the charity later? What if they didn't sell later? Does this policy ensure that the thrift shop has ample volunteers so they can keep the shop open and not pay employees? Were the volunteers putting their own interests before those of the charity?

Short-term vs. Long term

This is a "now versus later" dilemma that reflects the conflicts between immediate needs or wants and future goals. This question causes many heated discussions in companies when the need for short-term returns demanded by shareholders are in conflict with the long-term investment in product development that will insure the company's future. Protecting the environment for future generations is frequently in conflict with making and using convenient, inexpensive products today. Investing money in a retirement plan instead of buying a new car or home is a dilemma that many people face. These are not easy decisions.

✓ John was just accepted into the Executive MBA program at the prestigious university in his town. He was sponsored by his employer, who agreed to pay 50% of the tuition costs if John agreed to stay with the company for two years after he completed his degree. His employer had by-passed several other employees to open a promotion path for John. John was indebted to his employer for giving him the chance to excel. John was just about to sign on the dotted line, when he got a call from an executive recruiter on behalf of a major competitor who was offering him a position at a 20% salary increase. If he passed up the opportunity to attend the Executive MBA program he would disappoint his employer, burn a bridge with his colleagues and may never get another chance to attend the exclusive program. But with a house and two kids, the big jump in salary was much needed. Should he invest in his future or solidify his present?

Justice vs. Mercy

Justice pushes us towards decisions that are in line with our principles, keeping to the rules despite pressures of the situation of the moment, and pursuing fairness without considering personal situations. Mercy urges us towards bending the rules in order to care for the particular needs of an individual on a case-by-case basis, showing compassion, empathy, and generosity.

- ✓ Claire was the principal of an inner-city high school with limited resources. The school board had recently authorized the school to purchase laptop computers for each of the seniors on the condition that each student sign a document that he/she was personally responsible for the safe return of the computer at the end of the school year, or would be responsible for the cost of replacing the unit. Using the laptop would be critical to the ability of the students to graduate with the new curriculum the board had implemented. Half way through the first semester, Peter admitted to Claire that his computer had been stolen. Peter was a top student with strong potential to attend college and pull himself out of his impoverished neighborhood. Claire suspected that Peter's mother had stolen the computer to support her drug habit. Peter did not have the money to pay for the replacement so his graduation was in jeopardy. Peter's home situation was not very different from that of many of the students in the school. Should she uphold the rule and jeopardize Peter's future? If she made an exception, how should she handle similar situations with other students?

So how do you commit to doing the right thing? Rushworth Kidder (Kidder, 1995), outlines nine steps or checkpoints in order to offer a systematic way of dealing with issues of integrity and ethics.

1. *Recognize that there is a problem*. The first step is to acknowledge that there is a problem that deserves your time and attention. It requires that you elevate the issue in your mind rather than just push it aside.
2. *Determine the actor*. Find out who is responsible for addressing the problem. Keep in mind honoring your word includes what is expected of you in a proactive manner. What is your role in the problem? Where are your loyalties? What is your intention in addressing this problem?
3. *Gather the relevant facts*. Adequate, accurate, and current information about the situation is critical. Have you defined the problem correctly? How would you define the problem if you were on the other side? How did this situation develop and evolve? What was the cause of the problem, and what are the effects?
4. *Is this a "right versus wrong" decision*? Does the issue involve an action that is clearly illegal? Does the issue involve an action that is clearly immoral?
5. *Is this a "right versus right" decision*? Does the dilemma fall into one of the four categories: "truth versus loyalty," "individual versus community,"

"short-term versus long-term," or "justice versus mercy?"

6. *Apply the ethical standards and perspectives that match your core values.* In these grey areas of "right versus right" dilemmas, how will you evaluate the situation and decide in a way that meshes with your core values and honors your word? Some questions to consider:

   ✓ What is in the long-term best interest of the parties?
   ✓ What produces the greatest ratio of good to bad for each party? How do I maximize good?
   ✓ What would I want to have done if I were on the other side of this decision? The Golden Rule question.
   ✓ What do I wish everyone would do?
   ✓ What would I do if I wanted to fulfill my duties? If I have multiple duties, which is most critical?
   ✓ What would make the outcomes equal?
   ✓ What would make the outcome better for the less fortunate party?
   ✓ What decision creates the least negative outcome? How can I minimize harm?
   ✓ What decision most closely aligns with my personal core values? What decision most closely aligns with the core values of any organization that is involved?
   ✓ What are the possible unanticipated outcomes, both good and bad?
   ✓ What changes will happen in the future that could affect this decision now?

7. *Look for a third way.* Try to find a compromise between the positions that is a third option.

8. *Make the decision.* Leadership and moral courage must step in and enable you to make a decision.

9. *Revisit and reflect on the decision.* We learn from our choices. Did the outcome happen as you expected? What lessons can you learn to apply to future decisions? Would you make the same decision if the

facts were the same? If not, why not? How have you changed because of your decision? What have you learned from the process?

Integrity is like a three-legged stool. Legal standards, moral standards, and ethical standards (the ability to evaluate right versus right decisions) are the three legs of the stool. This foundation supports your ability to honor your word to yourself and to others.

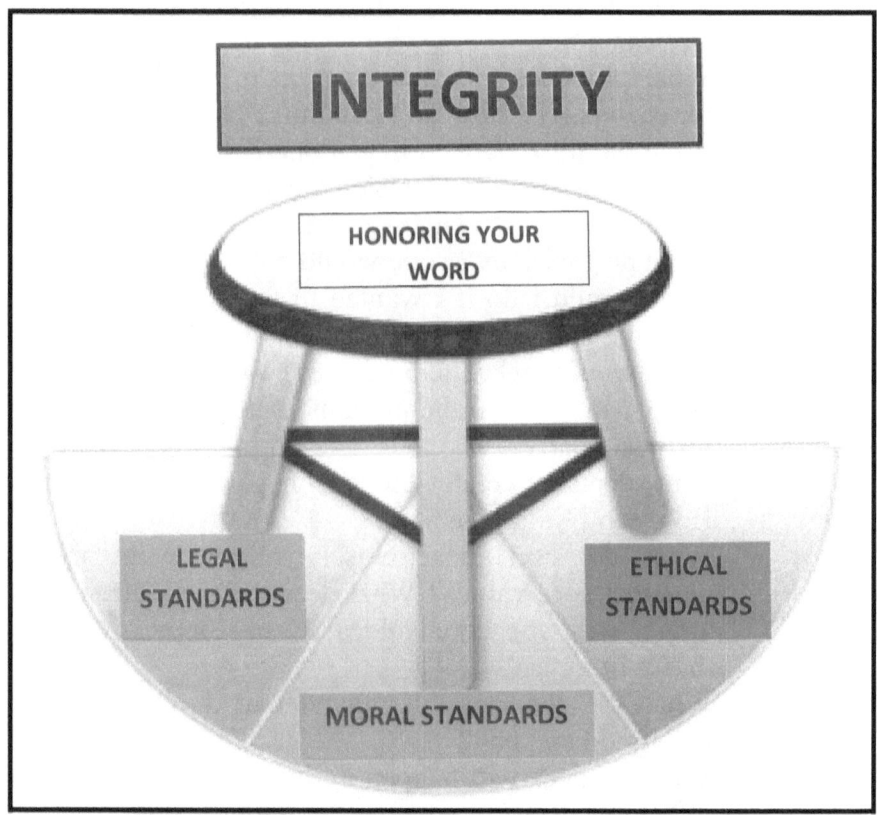

INTEGRITY

HONORING YOUR
WORD

LEGAL
STANDARDS

ETHICAL
STANDARDS

MORAL STANDARDS

EXERCISE IN DOING THE RIGHT THING

1. Begin with saying to yourself, "I am a person of integrity." Give yourself your word that you will act with integrity to yourself. When one's word to oneself is whole, complete, unbroken, unimpaired,

sound, and in perfect condition, it serves as a foundation on which one is likely to deal with one's word to others with integrity. Honoring your word to yourself is the basis of honoring your word to others. As Polonius said in Shakespeare's play, *Hamlet,* "This above all: to thine own self be true, And it must follow, as the night the day, Thou canst not then be false to any man." (Shakespeare)

2. Observe how you give your word to others. When you give your word to another, you create a new relationship, not only with the other individual but also with yourself. Give your word thoughtfully and with full commitment.

3. Select a situation that happened within the past few months that you felt you handled with integrity. Re-analyze it using the nine steps above. What would you have done differently? What did you do well? Would you still make the same decision? What did you learn about yourself and the others in the situation?

4. Select a situation that happened within the past few months that you felt you did not handle well, or where you felt your integrity slipped. Re-analyze it using the nine steps above. What would you do differently? What did you do well? Would you still make the same decision? What did you learn about yourself and the others in the situation?

Conclusion

Roomba® has integrity. It will fulfill its mission of cleaning my house whether or not I am in sight. In fact, I respect it more because I know I can count on it to honor it's word. When you honor your word to yourself and to others, you build a foundation of trust upon which all relationships will thrive. You owe it to yourself.

Chapter 10

Recharge your batteries before you can't make it back to the docking station

Last March, I came home from teaching an evening class and found my husband sitting on the sofa watching *American Idol*. He was shivering, huddled in a sweater, and was not fast-forwarding through the commercials. Something was wrong, really wrong. He looked dazed, and when I asked him why he didn't close the window if he was cold, he gave me the deer in the headlights look. He'd had a rough few months. He was facing some difficult challenges in his job, he had major surgery six weeks earlier, and the previous week his wonderful, 93-year-old father had passed away. He looked up at me and said woefully, "I didn't get back to the docking station in time." We immediately planned a long weekend in Cape Cod to recharge his batteries.

I have used Roomba® hundreds of times, in every room of my house. Every time I use it, it knows to head back to the docking station for recharging before it runs out of energy and collapses in the middle of the room. Small rooms, large rooms, it seems to know when to rest and recharge. Roomba® manages its energy, not its time. How smart!

If you are like me, you have read countless articles and books on time management, preventing burnout, and on increasing productivity in an organization. We are all trying to do more in less time, especially in hard economic times. How can we do what the "lazy person" would do; achieve more with less effort? Do what Roomba® does and manage your energy not your time. Are you getting back to the docking station before you drop from mental or physical exhaustion? What are you doing to monitor and renew your energy?

We all monitor the gas gauge on our cars. Right now, while reading this book, you probably know the approximate amount of fuel in your car and can estimate the distance to empty, without even looking. How are you monitoring your personal energy gauge? The first step is to understand what makes up your personal energy. In the book, *The Power of Full Engagement,* by Jim Loehr and Tony Schwartz (Loehr & Schwartz, 2005), and in the related article *Manage Your Energy, Not Your Time,* by Tony Schwartz and Catherine McCarthy (Schwartz & McCarthy, 2007), the authors describe four dimensions of personal energy: physical energy, emotional energy, mental energy, and spiritual energy. You need to have an energy gauge for each dimension. And, you need to recharge each before they are completely depleted.

PHYSICAL ENERGY

The ingredients in having physical energy are proper diet, effective exercise, sufficient sleep, and optimal physiological health. No surprises here. But too often the only treadmill we are on is the daily grind, not the one in the gym. Diet becomes the unplanned feast or famine, with an unbalanced ratio of carbohydrates and fat. Bragging about sleep deprivation has become a badge of honor in the workplace. We tend to one-ups-man with each other about how busy and stressful our schedules are.

PROPER DIET

HOW DO YOU MONITOR IT?	HOW DO YOU REFUEL IT?
Get a small notebook and write down everything you eat for two weeks, why you chose to eat that food at that particular time, and	"Treat" yourself to a trip to the best grocery store in your area, preferably one that specializes in organic or all-natural foods. Buy one item you have never tried

how you felt before and after eating it. Then, review it and look for patterns. Don't beat yourself up. Look at it as if you were analyzing someone else's data. Are you waiting to eat until you are absolutely starving, and will eat any junk food available? Are you eating too much just before bedtime? How are you handling those salty and sweet cravings? Are you eating when you are feeling stressed, anxious, or lonely? By doing this review, you will be aware of your diet landmines. It is likely that you will see that your hunger, energy level, and eating pattern looks like a giant sine wave. How do you expect to perform at peak levels all day when your calorie intake and metabolism pattern looks like ocean waves during a hurricane? You need to change your pattern so you are at metabolic balance.

Make a commitment to remove one of the landmines. Continue taking notes for two weeks, and then review to see how you are doing. Commit to removing another landmine. As you continue with the notebook, you will find that although you may occasionally step on a landmine, it will be a rare situation and your diet habits will be reformed in a better pattern.

before, and use it in a meal.

Have healthy snacks available, and take frequent small snack breaks during the day to keep your energy levels stable.

If you buy a "junk" food treat for yourself at the grocery store, buy the most expensive one. You will value it more and eat less of it.

Eat slowly, and cherish the flavor and aroma. Eating is fun, not something that should be done mindlessly.

Always eat a good breakfast to get your metabolism going.

Plan meals in advance, and look forward to the meals.

As you cook, pretend you have your own cooking show, turning a chore into a game.

Plan your food intake around your daily schedule. For example, if you are going to have a meeting that will run late into the evening, plan a more nutritious lunch and a small snack before the meeting with just a light snack after the meeting.

Brag to your colleagues about the great local produce you found, or the interesting grain you added to a salad. Change the culture in your organization to focus on healthy eating.

It's perhaps so simple and obvious that we forget about it, but hydration, drinking sufficient water, is key to maintaining health. Drink six to eight glasses of water each day.

EFFECTIVE EXERCISE

HOW DO YOU MONITOR IT?	HOW DO YOU REFUEL IT?
Every gym owner will agree that the busiest time in their business is January 1 to January 21 every year. New Year's Resolutions last about three weeks. Then everyone goes back to their "real" lives. Every person has an individual exercise requirement, in both the type and the extent. The consensus of experts is that thirty minutes per day of moderate activity is a minimum level to achieve. You need to find what will work for your body and your life. If you are an avid runner, tennis, or golf player, skip this part. But if you are like many of us, and let the demands of the job and family push out self time, then it's time to change. First, get that notebook out again and add a section on exercise. Record your exercise patterns for two weeks. Include brisk walks to and from parking lots, stairs, lawn care, gardening etc. Also record how you felt before and after the exercise. Remember to breathe deeply, and look for points of beauty along the way. Look for patterns of the type and extent of exercise that make you feel better. Commit to a plan to add similar activities each day. For example, take the stairs, park in the farthest space from your office, walk the dog twice a day. Up the ante bit by bit until you are getting a	Buy a pedometer and chart the number of steps you take each day. Set a specific goal for each week and reward yourself for reaching the goal. As you exercise, breathe deeply and let this be your personal time with no stress or worries. Try an experiment. The next time you have a difficult problem or a stressful event, step out of your workplace and take a five minute brisk walk. Think of the blood flowing faster, your heart beating quicker, and envision leaving the stress behind. This short break will let you see the issue with renewed vigor. Decide on a type of exercise that you will enjoy and not think of as "work." Start off slowly, so you find yourself looking forward to the activity, not dreading it. Make a commitment to yourself in writing. That makes it harder to not follow through. Give yourself small rewards that encourage exercise. Buy a new pair of walking shoes. Download a new music CD to accompany you on walks. Find a library that loans books on CD. Most

minimum of thirty minutes per day of moderate activity.	important, change your mindset. Exercise *is* fun.

SUFFICIENT SLEEP

HOW DO YOU MONITOR IT?	HOW DO YOU REFUEL IT?
Your notebook will become your best friend. Begin recording the number of hours you sleep and how you felt when you woke up. Then do the following test: 1. Set aside at least one week to focus on your sleep and not allow disruptions. Be sure that you can arrange for pets and children to be cared for. 2. Select a typical bedtime and stick with it each night. 3. Allow yourself to sleep in as long as you want, awakening without an alarm clock. 4. After a few days, you have paid off your sleep deficit and you will start to sleep the amount that your body needs. 5. After you determine the amount of sleep you need, then set your bedtime so that you can fit that amount into your night as often as possible. Remember that every individual is different; some need five hours and some need ten.	Set a schedule of a relaxing activity just before bedtime so you get yourself in the mood to enjoy sleeping. Reading a good book, a quiet conversation, or even a mindless TV show will do. If you find that you can't get your optimal amount of sleep for a few nights in a row, schedule a late morning so you can sleep in. Some individuals can recharge with quick power naps. If this works for you, make time for this. Be sure that your bedroom is quiet, comfortable, at the appropriate temperature, and very welcoming. Get a quality mattress and the most luxurious bed linens you can afford. Make bedtime something you look forward to instead of the necessary interlude between meetings. In the morning write down as much of your dreams as you can remember. Treasure the adventures of dreaming.

OPTIMAL PHYSIOLOGICAL HEALTH

HOW DO YOU MONITOR IT?	HOW DO YOU REFUEL IT?
Most of us routinely take our cars to the dealer with the schedule of suggested maintenance every 5,000 miles. Data supports the conclusion that if we follow the manufacturer's recommendations, the car will last longer, with fewer repair bills. Too bad humans don't come with a manufacturer's maintenance manual. You will have to write your own.	Find a primary physician who understands your goal of attaining optimal physical health, not just treatment of illness. Set physiological targets that are age-appropriate, monitor your progress to those targets, and reward yourself as you get to and stay at the goals. This is a hand-in-hand effort with your primary physician, and can include targets such as cholesterol levels, blood pressure, resting heart rate, and weight.
At the same time each year, set up your maintenance schedule. Good times to do this are January (a New Year's resolution), your birthday (so you can have many more) or September (the start of the school year always signifies renewal). Make a list of the routine maintenance you need: routine physical, round of blood tests, gynecological and mammogram exams for women, PSA screening for men, two dental checkups, and eye exams. Meet with your doctor to review the list and update it every year. Then make the appointments immediately. Put them on your calendar and treat them as unchangeable.	Studies have shown that individuals who are tuned in to their bodies notice symptoms earlier than those who ignore their physical health. Early recognition of "something different" leads to early detection and treatment of medical problems. The more tuned in to your body you are, the more you will notice small changes and be able to discuss those changes with your physician. You are the guardian of your body. Take that job seriously.

EMOTIONAL ENERGY

Has your get-up and-go gotten up and left? Do you drag yourself to do even the things you love to do? Your emotional energy tank may be empty. You need to replenish it. Mira Kirshenbaum, author of *The Emotional Energy Factor: The Secrets High-Energy People Use to Beat Emotional Fatigue* (Kirshenbaum, 2003), describes emotional energy as the energy that comes from being deeply connected to the fun and hope in life. She presents a diverse list of energy drains and energy boosters. My favorites are:

1. Do something new, anything, even a small thing, every week.
2. Always have something special in your life to look forward to.
3. Have at least a little bit of fun every day.
4. Stop regretting what can't be changed.
5. Bad things happen to everyone, but don't let your losses define you.
6. Be yourself, appreciate yourself, and stop making negative comparisons to others.
7. Pursue your passions.
8. Get rid of people-pollution. Stay away from those who drain your energy.
9. Embrace the present and look at the big picture.
10. Stop drowning in unfinished business. Give up worrying. Decide, and move on.

MENTAL ENERGY

Several years ago, I spent three weeks at a large corporation as a consultant for a strategic planning process. The corporate campus was gorgeous, and I especially loved the company-supported cafeteria. In the first week I had lunch with members of the team and most of our conversations were about the project. In the second week, the lunch table usually included employees from other parts of the company. By the third week, I had met over a hundred employees, and I dreaded lunch time. After the staff knew me well enough to "let their hair down," lunch conversations revolved around complaints, internal politics, work overload, high stress, and lack of appreciation by management. The negativity and unhappiness was overwhelming, and I could hear the clank of the golden handcuffs. I realized that no matter how good the strategic plan looked on paper, it would be difficult for this company to implement successfully. Negativity saps mental energy. Without mental energy, success will be difficult to achieve.

In the book, *The Happiness Advantage*, Shawn Achor (Achor, 2010) describes his research at Harvard University on the impact of happiness on measurable outcomes in business. In 2009, he consulted for the auditing and tax firm, KPMG, as they were about to go into the most stressful tax season in decades following the banking crises of 2008. Employees were evaluated three times, before the training, one week after training, and four months after training, using a battery of metrics, including life satisfaction measures, perceived stress, social support, perceived effectiveness at work, and work optimism. Every positive metric improved significantly, even four months after the training. The training involved five steps:

1. Write down three new things you are grateful for each day.
2. Write for two minutes a day describing one positive experience you had over the past 24 hours.
3. Exercise for ten minutes each day.
4. Meditate for two minutes each day, focusing on your breath going in and out.
5. Write one, quick email first thing in the morning thanking or praising a member of your team.

These simple assignments resulted in a retraining of the brain to focus on the positive, to look for points of happiness, and to express gratitude. Certainly worth a try.

SPIRITUAL ENERGY

A few years ago I was faced with a major decision that would affect me in every possible way. I had been approached by an investment company with an offer to acquire my business. After eighteen years of running the business as the sole owner, I had to admit to myself that I was beginning to smell burnout. But selling the business meant that I would have to be able to close one door and open another door in my life, stepping into the unknown. So I did what I so often did when I had to make an important decision, I went to the beach.

We were blessed to have a house at the New Jersey shore on the Delaware Bay, in a community called Del Haven, quiet, and surrounded by nature preserves. I spent a long weekend with my thoughts while looking at the water, the waves, the sand, and the tide changes. At high tide, the waves crested at the edge of our yard, but at low tide we could walk out about a half mile on the mud flats to reach the water's edge. At one point in the weekend, my husband turned to me and asked which I liked better, high tide or low tide. Actually, I loved them both. That was my moment of clarity. Running a business was high tide, waves crashing on my head 24/7. It was exhilarating, constantly changing, exciting, challenging, stressful, and consuming. I loved every minute of the eighteen years. After selling the business, life would be like low tide. The action would be at a distance. There would be time for peace, contemplation, reading, learning, helping others, and enjoying a more gentle life. It made me realize that the change was not giving up something but evolving to something different. One was not better than the other, just different.

For eighteen years I found spiritual energy and meaning in my life from growing a business, providing excellent products and services to a loyal customer base, providing jobs and opportunities for employees, and protecting the environment. The years since I sold the business have been filled with extraordinary spiritual energy and meaning from working in non-profit agencies, working to support the disabled community, spending more time with family and friends, assisting new entrepreneurs, and teaching. Spiritual energy is the "why" in life. Spiritual energy comes from acknowledging that you are part of a universe much bigger than yourself, and treasuring the role you play in that universe. It is knowing that you will leave a legacy, and actively mold the legacy that you leave.

When I present seminars to students, I frequently tell them the story of my father. He was born to Ukrainian immigrant parents, and began working as a foundry man in Bethlehem Steel Company at the age of ten. As a young child, I remember him coming home from work, covered in black soot, carrying his lunch pail and dropping into a chair from complete exhaustion. One day, I asked him what he did at work. He showed me a small bronze carving of a man pouring molten brass from a long handled ladle. He told me that he worked with the greatest group of men, who used their hearts and hands to create the parts that went on ships, planes, and in factories. He went on to say that their work keeps the country safe, builds planes that let people travel, and makes machines that are used to produce all kinds of stuff sold all over the world. He saw himself, not as a laborer in a hot, dirty, dangerous, low-paying, blue collar job, but as the creator of the finest brass parts in the world. His spiritual energy came from his vision and the legacy he was building.

Recently, I met a man, Dave, who, at age 61, could boast of over 35 years of experience selling flooring. He glows when he talks about wood laminate, tile, or vinyl flooring. He told me that he loves meeting with a new customer because he can give the customer the best solution to his flooring problem at the most affordable price. Dave saw himself, not as a salesman, but as an expert consultant helping customers to solve problems and beautify their properties with the most interesting and cost-effective products on the market.

I believe that Roomba® sees itself not as a motorized disk that sucks up dirt, but as the cutting edge of robotic technology with a mission of reducing dust, allergens, and debris from your home, to keep your family healthy and your property clean. How are you defining your work? Are you defining your work as sucking up dirt or as a protector of health and property?

What gives your work meaning? Ask yourself these questions.

- How does your work fit with and enhance your personal core values? If it doesn't, don't do it.
- Describe how your work in a team enhances the accomplishments of the team.
- List all the ways the world is better when you are done, even if that is just a little bit better.
- Give examples of how you touched someone in a positive way.
- Nobody does it better. Whatever you do, be the best. Describe your unique expertise.
- Look at the mission and vision of the organization. Write down why you believe in the mission, and what the organization will accomplish.
- Your work allows you to support yourself and your family. Make a list of things you and your family have been able to do because of the benefits of your employment.
- Work is fun. Describe ten things at work that are really fun.
- Work makes you think and be creative. What creative new idea can you add to your work that will make a difference this week?
- Describe what challenges you have at work. How do you feel when challenged? Describe the feelings when you succeed at a new challenge.
- What are the positive outcomes that you can achieve this week? This quarter? This year?
- What have you done to develop others? What have those individuals accomplished because of your support? What are you giving back to the next generation?
- Your work has given you resources to pursue other activities, hobbies, and travel. What have you been able to do because of your work?
- Where do you have independence, control, or autonomy, and how have you used these gifts to accomplish positive outcomes?

- Describe your meaningful relationships with co-workers, clients, vendors, and bosses. Think of the ways these people have enhanced your life.
- Describe how your work allows you the opportunity to learn and experience personal growth.
- Inventory your personal strengths, and describe how your work allows you to use those strengths. Describe a personal weakness and think of ways that in your work you can minimize that weakness, or even turn them into strengths.
- What are your natural talents? How does your work allow your natural talents to emerge and grow?
- Describe your personal passion. Describe how your work allows you to follow your passion.

Job descriptions don't have a section called "Meaning." Meaning is inside you. Look at yourself, at your personal motivations, goals, and desires, and then look at how your work fulfills them. Your challenge is to acknowledge meaning, and to maximize how your work creates personal meaning for you.

Be extraordinary!

Conclusion

Just as Roomba® returns to the docking station just in time, by monitoring its energy, not the time spent on the job, monitor and maximize your own personal energy. Monitor your physical, emotional, mental, and spiritual energy, and return to your personal docking station well before your battery runs down.

Chapter 11

Learn to Roomba® !

Here we are at the end of another book on leadership. People have been studying and writing about leadership for centuries. So, what's new? Not much. Researchers are continuing to analyze, and slice and dice, leadership traits. There are leadership books, seminars, training, and websites, all available to inundate us with the details of what makes a good leader. Yet, we are not overwhelmed with a high number of great leaders. Why are experts saying that "leadership training hasn't worked?" Because leadership is not easy. It is a choice, every day and in every situation. What makes us choose the leadership path?

- ✓ We have to know what the path looks like – read, listen, observe, learn.
- ✓ We accept that the leadership path is right.
- ✓ We want to choose the leadership path for ourselves – we commit.
- ✓ We constantly remind ourselves where the leadership path is, why we want to be on it, and how to be on it.

So, what's the most important lesson in the book? Yes, all of the above lessons are important, and I say that not because I wrote them down, but because they are documented steps to success. No, the most important message is to learn to open your mind to new ideas from the most unobvious sources. In this book, I used a household object, a vacuum cleaner, as a tool to remind us where the leadership path is. Heck, if a vacuum cleaner can be a leader, so can you.

We learned a lot from a vacuum cleaner. What can you learn from the items on your desk? The pencil – the eraser is there for a reason. Everybody makes mistakes, just use it and move on. The ball point pen – strive to do the crossword puzzle in ink – build your confidence. The coffee table – fill the gap between people with grace and beauty. The calendar – plan your life, not just your work. Open your mind!! LEARN!!

References

(2012). Retrieved from www.cleantheworld.org.

Achor, S. (2010). *The Happiness Advantage.* New York: Random House.

Alsop, R. (2008). *The Trophy Kids Grow Up: How the Millennial Generation is Shaking Up the Workplace.* San Francisco: Jossey-Bass.

Bryan, W. L., & Harter, N. (1897). Studies in the Physiology and Psychology of the Telegraphic Language. *Psychology Review* , 27-53.

Bryan, W. L., & Harter, N. (1899). Studies on the Telegraphic Language. The Acquisition of a Hierarchy of Habits. *Psychology Review* , 345-375.

Chodron, P. (2002). *Comfortable With Uncertainty: 108 Teachings on Cultivating Fearlessness and Compassion.* Boston, Ma: Shambhala Publishers, Inc.

Covey, S. R. (1989). *The 7 Habits of Highly Effective People.* New York: Simon & Schuster, Inc.

Demere, M. (2007, May 1). *So You Want to Be a Race Car Driver.* Retrieved 2012, from www.automedia.com: www.automedia.com

Dyke, L. S., & Murphy, S. A. (2006). How we define success: A Qualitative Study of What Matters Most to women and Men. *Sex Roles* , 55: 357-371.

Erhard, W. H., Jensen, M. C., & Zaffron, S. (2009). *Integrity: A Positive Model that Incorporates the Normative Phenomena of*

Morality, Ethics, and Legality. Retrieved 2012, from Landmark Education LLC: http://ssrn.com/abstract=920625

Ericsson, K. A., Charness, N., Feltovich, P. J., & Hoffman, R. R. (2006). *The Cambridge Handbook of Expertise and Expert Performance*. Cambridge UK: Cambridge University Press.

Ericsson, K. A., Prietula, M. J., & Cokely, E. T. (2007, July). The Making of an Expert. *Harvard Business Review*.

Falco, H. (2010). *I Am*. New York: Penguin Press.

Feldman, S. (2009). *The Male Factor*. New York: Random House.

Gawande, A. (2011, October 3). Personal Best. *The New Yorker*.

Gladwell, M. (2008). *Outliers The Story of Success*. New York: Little, Brown and Company.

Keller, F. (1958). The Phantom Plateau. *J. Exp. Anal. Behav.*

Kidder, R. M. (1995). *How Good People Make Tough Choices. Resolving the Dilemmas of Ethical Living*. New York: Harper Collins.

Kirshenbaum, M. (2003). *The Emotional Energy Factor: The Secrets High-Energy People Use to Beat Emotional Fatigue*. New York: Random House.

Langer, E. J. (2009). *Counter Clockwise Mindful Health and the Power of Possibility*. New York: Ballantine Books.

Langer, E. J. (1989). *Mindfulness*. Cambridge, Ma: Merloyd Lawrence Book.

Langer, E. J. (1997). *The Power of Mindful Learning*. Cambridge Ma: Merloyd Lawrence Book.

Loehr, J. (2008). *The Power of Story. Change your Story, Change your Destiny in Business and in Life*. New York: Free Press.

Loehr, J., & Schwartz, T. (2005). *the Power of Full Engagement.* New York: Free Press Paperbacks.

Marshall, G. (Director). (2011). *New Year's Eve* [Motion Picture].

Quindlen, A. (2012). *Lots of Candles Plenty of Cake.* New York: Random House.

Randy Pausch's website. (2007). Retrieved from Carnegie Mellon University: www.cs.cmu/pausch/

Schwartz, T., & McCarthy, C. (2007, October). Manage Your Energy, Not Your Time. *Harvard Business Review.*

Shakespeare, W. *Hamlet.* Act 1, Scene 3, 78-82.

Simonton, D. K. (2009). *Genius 101.* Springer Publlishing Company.

Tedeschi, R. G., & Calhoun, L. G. (2004). Post traumatic Growth: Conceptual Foundations and Empirical Evidence. *Psychological Inquiry* , 15, 1-18.

Tracy, B. (2001). *Eat That Frog!* San Fancisco: Berrett-Kochler Publishers, Inc.

Tulloss, R. (1918). *The Learning Curve. With Special Reference to the Progress of Students in Telegraphy and Typewriting.* Boston: Harvard University.

Twenge, J. M., & Campbell, W. K. (2009). *The Narcissism Epidemic. Living in the Age of Entitlement.* New York: Free Press.

Weingarten, G. (2007, April 8). Pearls Before Breakfast. *The Washington Post.*

Williams, R. (2010, July 18). *Wired for Success.* Retrieved 2012, from Psychology Today: www.psychologytoday.com

Wilson, H. J. (2012, April 2). Employees, Measure Yourself. *The Wall Street Journal* , pp. R1-R2.